IN A HOLLOW OF
THE HILLS

BRET HARTE

1st WORLD
LIBRARY
Literary Society

In a Hollow of the Hills

Bret Harte

© 1st World Library, 2007
PO Box 2211
Fairfield, IA 52556
www.1stworldlibrary.com
First Edition

LCCN: 2007934087

Softcover ISBN: 978-1-4218-9624-3
Hardcover ISBN: 978-1-4218-9724-0
eBook ISBN: 978-1-4218-9524-6

Purchase *"In a Hollow of the Hills"*
as a traditional bound book at:
www.1stWorldLibrary.com/purchase.asp?ISBN=978-1-4218-9624-3

1st World Library is a literary, educational organization
dedicated to:

- Creating a free internet library of downloadable ebooks

- Hosting writing competitions and offering book publishing
scholarships.

Interested in more 1st World Library books? contact:
literacy@1stworldlibrary.com
Check us out at: www.1stworldlibrary.com

1ˢᵗ World Library Literary Society

Giving Back to the World

"If you want to work on the core problem, it's early school literacy."

-James Barksdale, former CEO of Netscape

"No skill is more crucial to the future of a child, or to a democratic and prosperous society, than literacy."

-Los Angeles Times

"Literacy... means far more than learning how to read and write... The aim is to transmit... knowledge and promote social participation."

-UNESCO

"Literacy is not a luxury, it is a right and a responsibility. If our world is to meet the challenges of the twenty-first century we must harness the energy and creativity of all our citizens."

-President Bill Clinton

"Parents should be encouraged to read to their children, and teachers should be equipped with all available techniques for teaching literacy, so the varying needs and capacities of individual kids can be taken into account."

-Hugh Mackay

CHAPTER I

It was very dark, and the wind was increasing. The last gust had been preceded by an ominous roaring down the whole mountain-side, which continued for some time after the trees in the little valley had lapsed into silence. The air was filled with a faint, cool, sodden odor, as of stirred forest depths. In those intervals of silence the darkness seemed to increase in proportion and grow almost palpable. Yet out of this sightless and soundless void now came the tinkle of a spur's rowels, the dry crackling of saddle leathers, and the muffled plunge of a hoof in the thick carpet of dust and desiccated leaves. Then a voice, which in spite of its matter-of-fact reality the obscurity lent a certain mystery to, said:—

"I can't make out anything! Where the devil have we got to, anyway? It's as black as Tophet, here ahead!"

"Strike a light and make a flare with something," returned a second voice. "Look where you're shoving to—now—keep your horse off, will ye."

There was more muffled plunging, a silence, the rustle of paper, the quick spurt of a match, and then the uplifting of a flickering flame. But it revealed only the heads and shoulders of three horsemen, framed within a nebulous ring of light, that still left their horses and even their lower figures in impenetrable shadow. Then the flame leaped up and died out with a few zigzagging sparks that were falling to the ground, when a third voice, that was low but somewhat pleasant in its cadence, said:—

"Be careful where you throw that. You were careless last time. With this wind and the leaves like tinder, you might send a furnace blast through the woods."

"Then at least we'd see where we were."

Nevertheless, he moved his horse, whose trampling hoofs beat out the last fallen spark. Complete darkness and silence again followed. Presently the first speaker continued:—

"I reckon we'll have to wait here till the next squall clears away the scud from the sky? Hello! What's that?"

Out of the obscurity before them appeared a faint light,—a dim but perfectly defined square of radiance,—which, however, did not appear to illuminate anything around it. Suddenly it disappeared.

"That's a house—it's a light in a window," said the second voice.

"House be d—d!" retorted the first speaker. "A house with a window on Galloper's Ridge, fifteen miles from anywhere? You're crazy!"

Nevertheless, from the muffled plunging and tinkling that followed, they seemed to be moving in the direction where the light had appeared. Then there was a pause.

"There's nothing but a rocky outcrop here, where a house couldn't stand, and we're off the trail again," said the first speaker impatiently.

"Stop!—there it is again!"

The same square of light appeared once more, but the horsemen had evidently diverged in the darkness, for it seemed to be in a different direction. But it was more distinct, and as they gazed a shadow appeared upon its radiant surface—the profile of a human face. Then the light suddenly went out, and the face vanished with it.

"It IS a window, and there was some one behind it," said the second speaker emphatically.

"It was a woman's face," said the pleasant voice.

"Whoever it is, just hail them, so that we can get our bearings. Sing out! All together!"

The three voices rose in a prolonged shout, in which, however, the distinguishing quality of the pleasant voice was sustained. But there was no response from the darkness beyond. The shouting was repeated after an interval with the same result: the silence and obscurity remained unchanged.

"Let's get out of this," said the first speaker angrily; "house or no house, man or woman, we're not wanted, and we'll make nothing waltzing round here!"

"Hush!" said the second voice. "Sh-h! Listen."

The leaves of the nearest trees were trilling audibly. Then came a sudden gust that swept the fronds of the taller ferns into their faces, and laid the thin, lithe whips of alder over their horses' flanks sharply. It was followed by the distant sea-like roaring of the mountain-side.

"That's a little more like it!" said the first speaker joyfully. "Another blow like that and we're all right. And look! there's a lightenin' up over the trail we came by."

There was indeed a faint glow in that direction, like the first suffusion of dawn, permitting the huge shoulder of the mountain along whose flanks they had been journeying to be distinctly seen. The sodden breath of the stirred forest depths was slightly tainted with an acrid fume.

"That's the match you threw away two hours ago," said the pleasant voice deliberately. "It's caught the dry brush in the trail round the bend."

"Anyhow, it's given us our bearings, boys," said the first speaker, with satisfied accents. "We're all right now; and the wind's lifting the sky ahead there. Forward now, all together, and let's get out of this hell-hole while we can!"

It was so much lighter that the bulk of each horseman could be seen as they moved forward together. But there was no thinning of the obscurity on either side of them. Nevertheless the profile of the horseman with the pleasant voice seemed to be occasionally turned backward, and he suddenly checked his horse.

"There's the window again!" he said. "Look! There—it's gone again."

"Let it go and be d—d!" returned the leader. "Come on."

They spurred forward in silence. It was not long before the wayside trees began to dimly show spaces between them, and the ferns to give way to lower, thick-set shrubs, which in turn yielded to a velvety moss, with long quiet intervals of netted and tangled grasses. The regular fall of the horses' feet became a mere rhythmic throbbing. Then suddenly a single hoof rang out sharply on stone, and the first speaker reined in slightly.

"Thank the Lord we're on the ridge now! and the rest is easy. Tell you what, though, boys, now we're all right, I don't mind saying that I didn't take no stock in that blamed corpse light down there. If there ever was a will-o'-the-wisp on a square up mountain, that was one. It wasn't no window! Some of ye thought ye saw a face too—eh?"

"Yes, and a rather pretty one," said the pleasant voice meditatively.

"That's the way they'd build that sort of thing, of course. It's lucky ye had to satisfy yourself with looking. Gosh! I feel creepy yet, thinking of it! What are ye looking back for now like Lot's wife? Blamed if I don't think that face bewitched ye."

"I was only thinking about that fire you started," returned the other quietly. "I don't see it now."

"Well—if you did?"

"I was wondering whether it could reach that hollow."

"I reckon that hollow could take care of any casual nat'rel fire that came boomin' along, and go two better every time! Why, I don't believe there was any fire; it was all a piece of that infernal ignis fatuus phantasmagoriana that was played upon us down there!"

With the laugh that followed they started forward again, relapsing into the silence of tired men at the end of a long journey. Even their few remarks were interjectional, or reminiscent of topics whose freshness had been exhausted with the day. The gaining light which seemed to come from the ground about them rather than from the still, overcast sky above, defined their individuality more distinctly. The man who had first spoken, and who seemed to be their leader, wore the virgin unshaven beard, mustache, and flowing hair of the Californian pioneer, and might have been the eldest; the second speaker was close shaven, thin, and energetic; the third, with the pleasant voice, in height, litheness, and suppleness of figure appeared to be the youngest of the party. The trail had now become a grayish streak along the level table-land they were following, which also had the singular effect of appearing lighter than the surrounding landscape, yet of plunging into utter darkness on either side of its precipitous walls. Nevertheless, at the end of an hour the leader rose in his stirrups with a sigh of satisfaction.

"There's the light in Collinson's Mill! There's nothing gaudy and spectacular about that, boys, eh? No, sir! it's a square, honest beacon that a man can steer by. We'll be there in twenty minutes." He was pointing into the darkness below the already descending trail. Only a pioneer's eye could have detected the few pin-pricks of light in the impenetrable distance, and it was a signal proof of his leadership that the others accepted it without seeing it. "It's just ten o'clock," he continued, holding a huge silver watch to his eye; "we've wasted an hour on those blamed spooks yonder!"

"We weren't off the trail more than ten minutes, Uncle Dick," protested the pleasant voice.

"All right, my son; go down there if you like and fetch out your Witch of Endor, but as for me, I'm going to throw myself the other side of Collinson's lights. They're good enough for me, and a blamed sight more stationary!"

Bret Harte

The grade was very steep, but they took it, California fashion, at a gallop, being genuinely good riders, and using their brains as well as their spurs in the understanding of their horses, and of certain natural laws, which the more artificial riders of civilization are apt to overlook. Hence there was no hesitation or indecision communicated to the nervous creatures they bestrode, who swept over crumbling stones and slippery ledges with a momentum that took away half their weight, and made a stumble or false step, or indeed anything but an actual collision, almost impossible. Closing together they avoided the latter, and holding each other well up, became one irresistible wedge-shaped mass. At times they yelled, not from consciousness nor bravado, but from the purely animal instinct of warning and to combat the breathlessness of their descent, until, reaching the level, they charged across the gravelly bed of a vanished river, and pulled up at Collinson's Mill. The mill itself had long since vanished with the river, but the building that had once stood for it was used as a rude hostelry for travelers, which, however, bore no legend or invitatory sign. Those who wanted it, knew it; those who passed it by, gave it no offense.

Collinson himself stood by the door, smoking a contemplative pipe. As they rode up, he disengaged himself from the doorpost listlessly, walked slowly towards them, said reflectively to the leader, "I've been thinking with you that a vote for Thompson is a vote thrown away," and prepared to lead the horses towards the water tank. He had parted with them over twelve hours before, but his air of simply renewing a recently interrupted conversation was too common a circumstance to attract their notice. They knew, and he knew, that no one else had passed that way since he had last spoken; that the same sun had swung silently above him and the unchanged landscape, and there had been no interruption nor diversion to his monotonous thought. The wilderness annihilates time and space with the grim pathos of patience.

Nevertheless he smiled. "Ye don't seem to have got through coming down yet," he continued, as a few small boulders, loosened in their rapid descent, came more deliberately rolling and plunging after the travelers along the gravelly bottom. Then he turned away with the horses, and, after they were watered, he reentered the house. His guests had evidently not waited for his ministration. They had already taken one or two bottles from the shelves behind a wide bar and helped themselves, and, glasses in hand, were now satisfying the more imminent cravings of hunger with biscuits from a barrel and slices of smoked herring from a box. Their equally singular host, accepting their conduct as not unusual, joined the circle they had comfortably drawn round the fireplace, and meditatively kicking a brand back at the fire, said, without looking at them:—

"Well?"

"Well!" returned the leader, leaning back in his chair after carefully unloosing the buckle of his belt, but with his eyes also on the fire,—"well! we've prospected every yard of outcrop along the Divide, and there ain't the ghost of a silver indication anywhere."

"Not a smell," added the close-shaven guest, without raising his eyes.

They all remained silent, looking at the fire, as if it were the one thing they had taken into their confidence. Collinson also addressed himself to the blaze as he said presently: "It allus seemed to me that thar was something shiny about that ledge just round the shoulder of the spur, over the long canyon."

The leader ejaculated a short laugh. "Shiny, eh? shiny! Ye think THAT a sign? Why, you might as well reckon that because Key's head, over thar, is gray and silvery that he's got sabe and experience." As he spoke he looked towards the man with a pleasant voice. The fire shining full upon him revealed the singular fact that while his face was still young, and his mustache quite dark, his hair was perfectly gray. The object of this attention, far from being disconcerted by the comparison, added with a smile:—

"Or that he had any silver in his pocket."

Another lapse of silence followed. The wind tore round the house and rumbled in the short, adobe chimney.

"No, gentlemen," said the leader reflectively, "this sort o' thing is played out. I don't take no more stock in that cock-and-bull story about the lost Mexican mine. I don't catch on to that Sunday-school yarn about the pious, scientific sharp who collected leaves and vegetables all over the Divide, all the while he scientifically knew that the range was solid silver, only he wouldn't soil his fingers with God-forsaken lucre. I ain't saying anything agin that fine-spun theory that Key believes in about volcanic upheavals that set up on end argentiferous rock, but I simply say that I don't see it—with the naked eye. And I reckon it's about time, boys, as the game's up, that we handed in our checks, and left the board."

There was another silence around the fire, another whirl and turmoil without. There was no attempt to combat the opinions of their leader; possibly the same sense of disappointed hopes was felt by all, only they preferred to let the man of greater experience voice it. He went on:—

"We've had our little game, boys, ever since we left Rawlin's a week ago; we've had our ups and downs; we've been starved and parched, snowed up and half drowned, shot at by road-agents and horse-thieves, kicked by mules and played with by grizzlies. We've had a heap o' fun, boys, for our money, but I reckon the picnic is about over. So we'll shake hands to-morrow all round and call it square, and go on our ways separately."

"And what do you think you'll do, Uncle Dick?" said his close-shaven companion listlessly.

"I'll make tracks for a square meal, a bed that a man can comfortably take off his boots and die in, and some violet-scented soap. Civilization's good enough for me! I even reckon I wouldn't mind 'the sound of the church-going bell' ef there was a theatre handy, as there likely would be. But the wilderness is played out."

"You'll be back to it again in six months, Uncle Dick," retorted the other quickly.

Uncle Dick did not reply. It was a peculiarity of the party that in their isolated companionship they had already exhausted discussion and argument. A silence followed, in which they all looked at the fire as if it was its turn to make a suggestion.

"Collinson," said the pleasant voice abruptly, "who lives in the hollow this side of the Divide, about two miles from the first spur above the big canyon?"

"Nary soul!"

"Are you sure?"

"Sartin! Thar ain't no one but me betwixt Bald Top and Skinner's—twenty-five miles."

"Of course, YOU'D know if any one had come there lately?" persisted the pleasant voice.

"I reckon. It ain't a week ago that I tramped the whole distance that you fellers just rode over."

"There ain't," said the leader deliberately, "any enchanted castle or cabin that goes waltzing round the road with revolving windows and fairy princesses looking out of 'em?"

But Collinson, recognizing this as purely irrelevant humor, with possibly a trap or pitfall in it, moved away from the fireplace without a word, and retired to the adjoining kitchen to prepare supper. Presently he reappeared.

"The pork bar'l's empty, boys, so I'll hev to fix ye up with jerked beef, potatoes, and flapjacks. Ye see, thar ain't anybody ben over from Skinner's store for a week."

"All right; only hurry up!" said Uncle Dick cheerfully, settling himself back in his chair, "I reckon to turn in as soon as I've rastled with your hash, for I've got to turn out agin and be off at sun-up."

They were all very quiet again,—so quiet that they could not help noticing that the sound of Collinson's preparations for their supper had ceased too. Uncle Dick arose softly and walked to the kitchen door. Collinson was sitting before a small kitchen stove, with a fork in his hand, gazing abstractedly before him. At the sound of his guest's footsteps he started, and the noise of preparation recommenced. Uncle Dick returned to his chair by the fire. Leaning towards the chair of the close-shaven man, he said in a lower voice:—

"He was off agin!"

"What?"

"Thinkin' of that wife of his."

"What about his wife?" asked Key, lowering his voice also.

The three men's heads were close together.

"When Collinson fixed up this mill he sent for his wife in the States," said Uncle Dick, in a half whisper, "waited a year for her, hanging round and boarding every emigrant wagon that came through the Pass. She didn't come—only the news that she was dead." He paused and nudged his chair still closer—the heads were almost touching. "They say, over in the Bar"—his voice had sunk to a complete whisper—"that it was a lie! That she ran away with the man that was fetchin' her out. Three thousand miles and three weeks with another man upsets some women. But HE knows nothing about it, only he sometimes kinder goes off looney-like, thinking of her." He stopped, the heads separated; Collinson had appeared at the doorway, his melancholy patience apparently unchanged.

"Grub's on, gentlemen; sit by and eat."

The humble meal was dispatched with zest and silence. A few interjectional remarks about the uncertainties of prospecting only accented the other pauses. In ten minutes they were out again by the fireplace with their lit pipes. As there were only three chairs, Collinson stood beside the chimney.

"Collinson," said Uncle Dick, after the usual pause, taking his pipe from his lips, "as we've got to get up and get at sun-up, we might as well tell you now that we're dead broke. We've been living for the last few weeks on Preble Key's loose change—and that's gone. You'll have to let this little account and damage stand over."

Collinson's brow slightly contracted, without, however, altering his general expression of resigned patience.

"I'm sorry for you, boys," he said slowly, "and" (diffidently) "kinder sorry for myself, too. You see, I reckoned on goin' over to Skinner's to-morrow, to fill up the pork bar'l and vote for Mesick and the wagon-road. But Skinner can't let me have anything more until I've paid suthin' on account, as he calls it."

"D'ye mean to say thar's any mountain man as low flung and mean as that?" said Uncle Dick indignantly.

"But it isn't HIS fault," said Collinson gently; "you see, they won't send him goods from Sacramento if he don't pay up, and he CAN'T if I DON'T. Sabe?"

"Ah! that's another thing. They ARE mean—in Sacramento," said Uncle Dick, somewhat mollified.

The other guests murmured an assent to this general proposition. Suddenly Uncle Dick's face brightened.

"Look here! I know Skinner, and I'll stop there—No, blank it all! I can't, for it's off my route! Well, then, we'll fix it this way. Key will go there and tell Skinner that I say that I'LL send the money to that Sacramento hound. That'll fix it!"

Collinson's brow cleared; the solution of the difficulty seemed to satisfy everybody, and the close-shaven man smiled.

"And I'll secure it," he said, "and give Collinson a sight draft on myself at San Francisco."

"What's that for?" said Collinson, with a sudden suffusion on each cheek.

"In case of accident."

"Wot accident?" persisted Collinson, with a dark look of suspicion on his usually placid face.

"In case we should forget it," said the close-shaven man, with a laugh.

"And do you suppose that if you boys went and forgot it that I'd have anything to do with your d—d paper?" said Collinson, a murky cloud coming into his eyes.

"Why, that's only business, Colly," interposed Uncle Dick quickly; "that's all Jim Parker means; he's a business man, don't you see. Suppose we got killed! You've that draft to show."

"Show who?" growled Collinson.

"Why,—hang it!—our friends, our heirs, our relations—to get your money, hesitated Uncle Dick.

"And do you kalkilate," said Collinson, with deeply laboring breath, "that if you got killed, that I'd be coming on your folks for the worth of the d—d truck I giv ye? Go 'way! Lemme git out o' this. You're makin' me tired." He stalked to the door, lit his pipe, and began to walk up and down the gravelly river-bed. Uncle Dick followed him. From time to time the two other guests heard the sounds of alternate protest and explanation as they passed and repassed the windows. Preble Key smiled, Parker shrugged his shoulders.

"He'll be thinkin' you've begrudged him your grub if you don't—that's the way with these business men," said Uncle Dick's voice in one of these intervals. Presently they reentered the house, Uncle Dick saying casually to Parker, "You can leave that draft on the bar when you're ready to go to-morrow;" and the incident was presumed to have ended. But Collinson did not glance in the direction of Parker for the rest of the evening; and, indeed, standing with his back to the chimney, more than once fell into that stolid abstraction which was supposed to be the contemplation of his absent wife.

From this silence, which became infectious, the three guests were suddenly aroused by a furious clattering down the steep descent of the mountain, along the trail they had just ridden! It came near, increasing in sound, until it even seemed to scatter the fine gravel of the river-bed against the sides of the house, and then passed in a gust of wind that shook the roof and roared in the chimney. With one common impulse the three travelers rose and went to the door. They opened it to a blackness that seemed to stand as another and an iron door before them, but to nothing else.

"Somebody went by then," said Uncle Dick, turning to Collinson. "Didn't you hear it?"

"Nary," said Collinson patiently, without moving from the chimney.

"What in God's name was it, then?"

"Only some of them boulders you loosed coming down. It's touch and go with them for days after. When I first came here I used to start up and rush out into the road—like as you would—yellin' and screechin' after folks that never was there and never went by. Then it got kinder monotonous, and I'd lie still and let 'em slide. Why, one night I'd a'sworn that some one pulled up with a yell and shook the door. But I sort of allowed to myself that whatever it was, it wasn't wantin' to eat, drink, sleep, or it would come in, and I hadn't any call to interfere. And in the mornin' I found a rock as big as that box, lying chock-a-block agin the door. Then I knowed I was right."

Preble Key remained looking from the door.

"There's a glow in the sky over Big Canyon," he said, with a meaning glance at Uncle Dick.

"Saw it an hour ago," said Collinson. "It must be the woods afire just round the bend above the canyon. Whoever goes to Skinner's had better give it a wide berth."

Key turned towards Collinson as if to speak, but apparently changed his mind, and presently joined his companions, who were already rolling themselves in their blankets, in a series of wooden bunks or berths, ranged as in a ship's cabin, around the walls of a resinous, sawdusty apartment that had been the measuring room of the mill. Collinson disappeared,—no one knew or seemed to care where,—and, in less than ten minutes from the time that they had returned from the door, the hush of sleep and rest seemed to possess the whole house. There was no light but that of the fire in the front room, which threw flickering and gigantic shadows on the walls of the three empty chairs before it. An hour later it seemed as if one of the chairs were occupied, and a grotesque profile of Collinson's slumbering—or meditating—face and figure was projected grimly on the rafters as though it were the hovering guardian spirit of the house. But even that passed presently and faded out, and the beleaguering darkness that had encompassed the house all the evening began to slowly creep in through every chink and cranny of the rambling, ill-jointed structure, until it at last obliterated even the faint embers on the hearth. The cool fragrance of the woodland depths crept in with it until the steep of human warmth, the reek of human clothing, and the lingering odors of stale human victual were swept away in that incorruptible and omnipotent breath. An hour later—and the wilderness had repossessed itself of all.

Key, the lightest sleeper, awoke early,—so early that the dawn announced itself only in two dim squares of light that seemed to grow out of the darkness at the end of the room where the windows looked out upon the valley. This reminded him of his woodland vision of the night before, and he lay and watched them until they brightened and began to outline the figures of his still sleeping companions. But there were faint stirrings elsewhere,—the soft brushing of a squirrel across the shingled roof, the tiny flutter of invisible wings in the rafters, the "peep" and "squeak" of baby life below the floor. And then he fell into a deeper sleep, and awoke only when it was broad day.

The sun was shining upon the empty bunks; his companions were already up and gone. They had separated as they had come together,—with the light-hearted irresponsibility of animals,—without regret, and scarcely reminiscence; bearing, with cheerful philosophy and the hopefulness of a future unfettered by their past, the final disappointment of their quest. If they ever met again, they would laugh and remember; if they did not, they would forget without a sigh. He hurriedly dressed himself, and went outside to dip his face and hands in the bucket that stood beside the door; but the clear air, the dazzling sunshine, and the unexpected prospect half intoxicated him.

The abandoned mill stretched beside him in all the pathos of its premature decay. The ribs of the water-wheel appeared amid a tangle of shrubs and driftwood, and were twined with long grasses and straggling vines; mounds of sawdust and heaps of "brush" had taken upon themselves a velvety moss where the trickling slime of the vanished river lost itself in sluggish pools, discolored with the dyes of redwood. But on the other side of the rocky ledge dropped the whole length of the valley, alternately bathed in sunshine or hidden in drifts of white and clinging smoke. The upper end of the long canyon, and the crests of the ridge above him, were lost in this fleecy cloud, which at times seemed to overflow the summits and fall in slow leaps like lazy cataracts down the mountain-side. Only the range before the ledge was clear; there the green pines seemed to swell onward and upward in long mounting billows, until at last they broke against the sky.

In the keen stimulus of the hour and the air Key felt the mountaineer's longing for action, and scarcely noticed that Collinson had pathetically brought out his pork barrel to scrape together a few remnants for his last meal. It was not until he had finished his coffee, and Collinson had brought up his horse, that a slight sense of shame at his own and his comrades' selfishness embarrassed his parting with his patient host. He himself was going to Skinner's to plead for him; he knew that Parker had left the draft,—he had seen it lying in the bar,—but a new sense of delicacy kept him from alluding to it now. It was better to leave Collinson with his own peculiar ideas of the responsibilities of hospitality unchanged. Key shook his hand warmly, and galloped up the rocky slope. But when he had finally reached the higher level, and fancied he could even now see the dust raised by his departing comrades on their two diverging paths, although he knew that they had already gone their different ways,—perhaps never to meet again,—his thoughts and his eyes reverted only to the ruined mill below him and its lonely occupant.

He could see him quite distinctly in that clear air, still standing before his door. And then he appeared to make a parting gesture with his hand, and something like snow fluttered in the air above his head. It was only the torn fragments of Parker's draft, which this homely gentleman of the Sierras, standing beside his empty pork barrel, had scattered to the four winds.

CHAPTER II

Key's attention was presently directed to something more important to his present purpose. The keen wind which he had faced in mounting the grade had changed, and was now blowing at his back. His experience of forest fires had already taught him that this was too often only the cold air rushing in to fill the vacuum made by the conflagration, and it needed not his sensation of an acrid smarting in his eyes, and an unaccountable dryness in the air which he was now facing, to convince him that the fire was approaching him. It had evidently traveled faster than he had expected, or had diverged from its course. He was disappointed, not because it would oblige him to take another route to Skinner's, as Collinson had suggested, but for a very different reason. Ever since his vision of the preceding night, he had resolved to revisit the hollow and discover the mystery. He had kept his purpose a secret,—partly because he wished to avoid the jesting remarks of his companions, but particularly because he wished to go alone, from a very singular impression that although they had witnessed the incident he had really seen more than they did. To this was also added the haunting fear he had felt during the night that this mysterious habitation and its occupants were in the track of the conflagration. He had not dared to dwell upon it openly on account of Uncle Dick's evident responsibility for the origin of the fire; he appeased his conscience with the reflection that the inmates of the dwelling no doubt had ample warning in time to escape. But still, he and his companions ought to have stopped to help them, and then—but here he paused, conscious of another reason he could scarcely voice then, or even now. Preble Key had not passed the age of romance, but like other romancists he thought he had evaded it by treating it practically.

Meantime he had reached the fork where the trail diverged to the right, and he must take that direction if he wished to make a detour of the burning woods to reach Skinner's. His momentary indecision communicated itself to his horse, who halted. Recalled to himself, he looked down mechanically, when his attention was attracted by an unfamiliar object lying in the dust of the trail. It was a small slipper—so small that at first he thought it must have belonged to some child. He dismounted and picked it up. It was worn and shaped to the foot. It could not have lain there long, for it was not filled nor discolored by the wind-blown dust of the trail, as all other adjacent objects were. If it had been dropped by a passing traveler, that traveler must have passed Collinson's, going or coming, within the last twelve hours. It was scarcely possible that the shoe could have dropped from the foot without the wearer's knowing it, and it must have been dropped in an urgent flight, or it would have been recovered. Thus practically Key treated his romance. And having done so, he instantly wheeled his horse and plunged into the road in the direction of the fire.

But he was surprised after twenty minutes' riding to find that the course of the fire had evidently changed. It was growing clearer before him; the dry heat seemed to come more from the right, in the direction of the detour he should have taken to Skinner's. This seemed almost providential, and in keeping with his practical treatment of his romance, as was also the fact that in all probability the fire had not yet visited the little hollow which he intended to explore. He knew he was nearing it now; the locality had been strongly impressed upon him even in the darkness of the previous evening. He had passed the rocky ledge; his horse's hoofs no longer rang out clearly; slowly and perceptibly they grew deadened in the springy mosses, and were finally lost in the netted grasses and tangled vines that indicated the vicinity of the densely wooded hollow. Here were already some of the wider spaced vanguards of that wood; but here, too, a peculiar circumstance struck him. He was already descending the slight declivity; but the distance, instead of deepening in leafy shadow, was actually growing lighter. Here were the outskirting sentinels of the wood—but the wood itself was gone! He spurred his horse through the tall arch between the opened columns, and pulled up in amazement.

The wood, indeed, was gone, and the whole hollow filled with the already black and dead stumps of the utterly consumed forest! More than that, from the indications before him, the catastrophe must have almost immediately followed his retreat from the hollow on the preceding night. It was evident that the fire had leaped the intervening shoulder of the spur in one of the unaccountable, but by no means rare, phenomena of this kind of disaster. The circling heights around were yet untouched; only the hollow, and the ledge of rock against which they had blundered with their horses when they were seeking the mysterious window in last evening's darkness, were calcined and destroyed. He dismounted and climbed the ledge, still warm from the spent fire. A large mass of grayish outcrop had evidently been the focus of the furnace blast of heat which must have raged for hours in this spot. He was skirting its crumbling debris when he started suddenly at a discovery which made everything else fade into utter insignificance. Before him, in a slight depression formed by a fault or lapse in the upheaved strata, lay the charred and incinerated remains of a dwelling-house leveled to the earth! Originally half hidden by a natural abattis of growing myrtle and ceanothus which covered this counter-scarp of rock towards the trail, it must have stood within a hundred feet of them during their halt!

Even in its utter and complete obliteration by the furious furnace blast that had swept across it, there was still to be seen an unmistakable ground plan and outline of a four-roomed house. While everything that was combustible had succumbed to that intense heat, there was still enough half-fused and warped metal, fractured iron plate, and twisted and broken bars to indicate the kitchen and tool shed. Very little had, evidently, been taken away; the house and its contents were consumed where they stood. With a feeling of horror and desperation Key at last ventured to disturb two or three of the blackened heaps that lay before him. But they were only vestiges of clothing, bedding, and crockery—there was no human trace that he could detect. Nor was there any suggestion of the original condition and quality of the house, except its size: whether the ordinary unsightly cabin of frontier "partners," or some sylvan cottage—there was nothing left but the usual ignoble and unsavory ruins of burnt-out human habitation.

And yet its very existence was a mystery. It had been unknown at Collinson's, its nearest neighbor, and it was presumable that it was equally unknown at Skinner's. Neither he nor his companions had detected it in their first journey by day through the hollow, and only the tell-tale window at night had been a hint of what was even then so successfully concealed that they could not discover it when they had blundered against its rock foundation. For concealed it certainly was, and intentionally so. But for what purpose?

He gave his romance full play for a few minutes with this question. Some recluse, preferring the absolute simplicity of nature, or perhaps wearied with the artificialities of society, had secluded himself here with the company of his only daughter. Proficient as a pathfinder, he had easily discovered some other way of provisioning his house from the settlements than by the ordinary trails past Collinson's or Skinner's, which would have betrayed his vicinity. But recluses are not usually accompanied by young daughters, whose relations with the world, not being as antagonistic, would make them uncertain companions. Why not a wife? His presumption of the extreme youth of the face he had seen at the window was after all only based upon the slipper he had found. And if a wife, whose absolute acceptance of such confined seclusion might be equally uncertain, why not somebody else's wife? Here was a reason for concealment, and the end of an episode, not unknown even in the wilderness. And here was the work of the Nemesis who had overtaken them in their guilty contentment! The story, even to its moral, was complete. And yet it did not entirely satisfy him, so superior is the absolutely unknown to the most elaborate theory.

His attention had been once or twice drawn towards the crumbling wall of outcrop, which during the conflagration must have felt the full force of the fiery blast that had swept through the hollow and spent its fury upon it. It bore evidence of the intense heat in cracked fissures and the crumbling debris that lay at its feet. Key picked up some of the still warm fragments, and was not surprised that they easily broke in a gritty, grayish powder in his hands. In spite of his preoccupation with the human interest, the instinct of the prospector was still strong upon him, and he almost mechanically put some of the pieces in his pockets. Then after another careful survey of the locality for any further record of its vanished tenants, he returned to his horse. Here he took from his saddle-bags, half listlessly, a precious phial encased in wood, and, opening it, poured into another thick glass vessel part of a smoking fluid; he then crumbled some of the calcined fragments into the glass, and watched the ebullition that followed with mechanical gravity. When it had almost ceased he drained off the contents into another glass, which he set down, and then proceeded to pour some water from his drinking-flask into the ordinary tin cup which formed part of his culinary traveling-kit. Into this he put three or four pinches of salt from his provision store. Then dipping his fingers into the salt and water, he allowed a drop to fall into the glass. A white cloud instantly gathered in the colorless fluid, and then fell in a fine film to the bottom of the glass. Key's eyes concentrated suddenly, the listless look left his face. His fingers trembled lightly as he again let the salt water fall into the solution, with exactly the same result! Again and again he repeated it, until the bottom of the glass was quite gray with the fallen precipitate. And his own face grew as gray.

His hand trembled no longer as he carefully poured off the solution so as not to disturb the precipitate at the bottom. Then he drew out his knife, scooped a little of the gray sediment upon its point, and emptying his tin cup, turned it upside down upon his knee, placed the sediment upon it, and began to spread it over the dull surface of its bottom with his knife. He had intended to rub it briskly with his knife blade. But in the very action of spreading it, the first stroke of his knife left upon the sediment and the cup the luminous streak of burnished silver!

He stood up and drew a long breath to still the beatings of his heart. Then he rapidly re-climbed the rock, and passed over the ruins again, this time plunging hurriedly through, and kicking aside the charred heaps without a thought of what they had contained. Key was not an unfeeling man, he was not an unrefined one: he was a gentleman by instinct, and had an intuitive sympathy for others; but in that instant his whole mind was concentrated upon the calcined outcrop! And his first impulse was to see if it bore any evidence of previous examination, prospecting, or working by its suddenly evicted neighbors and owners. There was none: they had evidently not known it. Nor was there any reason to suppose that they would ever return to their hidden home, now devastated and laid bare to the open sunlight and open trail. They were already far away; their guilty personal secret would keep them from revisiting it. An immense feeling of relief came over the soul of this moral romancer; a momentary recognition of the Most High in this perfect poetical retribution. He ran back quickly to his saddle-bags, drew out one or two carefully written, formal notices of preemption and claim, which he and his former companions had carried in their brief partnership, erased their signatures and left only his own name, with another grateful sense of Divine interference, as he thought of them speeding far away in the distance, and returned to the ruins. With unconscious irony, he selected a charred post from the embers, stuck it in the ground a few feet from the debris of outcrop, and finally affixed his "Notice." Then, with a conscientiousness born possibly of his new religious convictions, he dislodged with his pickaxe enough of the brittle outcrop to constitute that presumption of "actual work" upon the claim which was legally required for its maintenance, and returned to his horse. In replacing his things in his saddle-bags he came upon the slipper, and for an instant so complete was his preoccupation in his later discovery, that he was about to throw it away as useless impedimenta, until it occurred to him, albeit vaguely, that it might be of service to him in its connection with that discovery, in the way of refuting possible false claimants. He was not aware of any faithlessness to his momentary romance, any more than he was conscious of any disloyalty to his old companions, in his gratification that his good fortune had come to him alone. This singular selection was a common experience of prospecting. And there was something about the magnitude of his discovery that seemed to point to an individual achievement. He had made a rough calculation of the richness of the lode from the quantity of precipitate in his rude experiment; he had estimated its length, breadth, and thickness from his slight knowledge of geology and the theories then ripe; and the yield would be colossal! Of course, he would require capital to work it, he would have to "let in" others to his scheme and his prosperity; but the control of it would always be HIS OWN.

Then he suddenly started as he had never in his life before started at the foot of man! For there was a footfall in the charred brush; and not twenty yards from him stood Collinson, who had just dismounted from a mule. The blood rushed to Key's pale face.

"Prospectin' agin?" said the proprietor of the mill, with his weary smile.

"No," said Key quickly, "only straightening my pack." The blood deepened in his cheek at his instinctive lie. Had he carefully thought it out before, he would have welcomed Collinson, and told him all. But now a quick, uneasy suspicion flashed upon him. Perhaps his late host had lied, and knew of the existence of the hidden house. Perhaps—he had spoken of some "silvery rock" the night before—he even knew something of the lode itself. He turned upon him with an aggressive face. But Collinson's next words dissipated the thought.

"I'm glad I found ye, anyhow," he said. "Ye see, arter you left, I saw ye turn off the trail and make for the burning woods instead o' goin' round. I sez to myself, 'That fellow is making straight for Skinner's. He's sorter worried about me and that empty pork bar'l,'—I hadn't oughter spoke that away afore you boys, anyhow,—'and he's takin' risks to help me.' So I reckoned I'd throw my leg over Jenny here, and look arter ye—and go over to Skinner's myself—and vote."

"Certainly," said Key with cheerful alacrity, and the one thought of getting Collinson away; "we'll go together, and we'll see that that pork barrel is filled!" He glowed quite honestly with this sudden idea of remembering Collinson through his good fortune. "Let's get on quickly, for we may find the fire between us on the outer trail." He hastily mounted his horse.

"Then you didn't take this as a short cut," said Collinson, with dull perseverance in his idea. "Why not? It looks all clear ahead."

"Yes," said Key hurriedly, "but it's been only a leap of the fire, it's still raging round the bend. We must go back to the cross-trail." His face was still flushing with his very equivocating, and his anxiety to get his companion away. Only a few steps further might bring Collinson before the ruins and the "Notice," and that discovery must not be made by him until Key's plans were perfected. A sudden aversion to the man he had a moment before wished to reward began to take possession of him. "Come on," he added almost roughly.

But to his surprise, Collinson yielded with his usual grim patience, and even a slight look of sympathy with his friend's annoyance. "I reckon you're right, and mebbee you're in a hurry to get to Skinner's all along o' MY business, I oughtn't hev told you boys what I did." As they rode rapidly away he took occasion to add, when Key had reined in slightly, with a feeling of relief at being out of the hollow, "I was thinkin', too, of what you'd asked about any one livin' here unbeknownst to me."

"Well," said Key, with a new nervousness.

"Well; I only had an idea o' proposin' that you and me just took a look around that holler whar you thought you saw suthin'!" said Collinson tentatively.

"Nonsense," said Key hurriedly. "We really saw nothing—it was all a fancy; and Uncle Dick was joking me because I said I thought I saw a woman's face," he added with a forced laugh.

Collinson glanced at him, half sadly. "Oh! You were only funnin', then. I oughter guessed that. I oughter have knowed it from Uncle Dick's talk!" They rode for some moments in silence; Key preoccupied and feverish, and eager only to reach Skinner's. Skinner was not only postmaster but "registrar" of the district, and the new discoverer did not feel entirely safe until he had put his formal notification and claims "on record." This was no publication of his actual secret, nor any indication of success, but was only a record that would in all probability remain unnoticed and unchallenged amidst the many other hopeful dreams of sanguine prospectors. But he was suddenly startled from his preoccupation.

"Ye said ye war straightenin' up yer pack just now," said Collinson slowly.

"Yes!" said Key almost angrily, "and I was."

"Ye didn't stop to straighten it up down at the forks of the trail, did ye?"

"I may have," said Key nervously. "But why?"

"Ye won't mind my axin' ye another question, will ye? Ye

ain't carryin' round with ye no woman's shoe?"

Key felt the blood drop from his cheeks. "What do you mean?" he stammered, scarcely daring to lift his conscious eyelids to his companion's glance. But when he did so he was amazed to find that Collinson's face was almost as much disturbed as his own.

"I know it ain't the square thing to ask ye, but this is how it is," said Collinson hesitatingly. "Ye see just down by the fork of the trail where you came I picked up a woman's shoe. It sorter got me! For I sez to myself, 'Thar ain't no one bin by my shanty, comin' or goin', for weeks but you boys, and that shoe, from the looks of it, ain't bin there as many hours.' I knew there wasn't any wimin hereabouts. I reckoned it couldn't hev bin dropped by Uncle Dick or that other man, for you would have seen it on the road. So I allowed it might have bin YOU. And yer it is." He slowly drew from his pocket—what Key was fully prepared to see—the mate of the slipper Key had in his saddle-bags! The fair fugitive had evidently lost them both.

But Key was better prepared now (perhaps this kind of dissimulation is progressive), and quickly alive to the necessity of throwing Collinson off this unexpected scent. And his companion's own suggestion was right to his hand, and, as it seemed, again quite providential! He laughed, with a quick color, which, however, appeared to help his lie, as he replied half hysterically, "You're right, old man, I own up, it's mine! It's d—d silly, I know—but then, we're all fools where women are concerned—and I wouldn't have lost that slipper for a mint of money."

He held out his hand gayly, but Collinson retained the slipper while he gravely examined it.

"You wouldn't mind telling me where you mought hev got that?" he said meditatively.

"Of course I should mind," said Key with a well-affected mingling of mirth and indignation. "What are you thinking of, you old rascal? What do you take me for?"

But Collinson did not laugh. "You wouldn't mind givin' me the size and shape and general heft of her as wore that shoe?"

"Most decidedly I should do nothing of the kind!" said Key half impatiently. "Enough, that it was given to me by a very pretty girl. There! that's all you will know."

"GIVEN to you?" said Collinson, lifting his eyes.

"Yes," returned Key sharply.

Collinson handed him the slipper gravely. "I only asked you," he said slowly, but with a certain quiet dignity which Key had never before seen in his face, "because thar was suthin' about the size, and shape, and fillin' out o' that shoe that kinder reminded me of some 'un; but that some 'un—her as mought hev stood up in that shoe—ain't o' that kind as would ever stand in the shoes of her as YOU know at all." The rebuke, if such were intended, lay quite as much in the utter ignoring of Key's airy gallantry and levity as in any conscious slur upon the fair fame of his invented Dulcinea. Yet Key oddly felt a strong inclination to resent the aspersion as well as Collinson's gratuitous morality; and with a mean recollection of Uncle Dick's last evening's scandalous gossip, he said sarcastically, "And, of course, that some one YOU were thinking of was your lawful wife."

"It war!" said Collinson gravely.

Perhaps it was something in Collinson's manner, or his own preoccupation, but he did not pursue the subject, and the conversation lagged. They were nearing, too, the outer edge of the present conflagration, and the smoke, lying low in the unburnt woods, or creeping like an actual exhalation of the soil, blinded them so that at times they lost the trail completely. At other times, from the intense heat, it seemed as if they were momentarily impinging upon the burning area, or were being caught in a closing circle. It was remarkable that with his sudden accession of fortune Key seemed to lose his usual frank and careless fearlessness, and impatiently questioned his companion's woodcraft. There were intervals when he regretted his haste to reach Skinner's by this shorter cut, and began to bitterly attribute it to his desire to serve Collinson. Ah, yes! it would be fine indeed, if just as he were about to clutch the prize he should be sacrificed through the ignorance and stupidity of this heavy-handed moralist at his side! But it was not until, through that moralist's guidance, they climbed a steep acclivity to a second ridge, and were comparatively safe, that he began to feel ashamed of his surly silence or surlier interruptions. And Collinson, either through his unconquerable patience, or possibly in a fit of his usual uxorious abstraction, appeared to take no notice of it.

A sloping table-land of weather-beaten boulders now effectually separated them from the fire on the lower ridge. They presently began to descend on the further side of the crest, and at last dropped upon a wagon-road, and the first track of wheels that Key had seen for a fortnight. Rude as it was, it seemed to him the highway to fortune, for he knew that it passed Skinner's and then joined the great stage-road to Marysville,—now his ultimate destination. A few rods further on they came in view of Skinner's, lying like a dingy forgotten winter snowdrift on the mountain shelf.

It contained a post-office, tavern, blacksmith's shop, "general store," and express-office, scarcely a dozen buildings in all, but all differing from Collinson's Mill in some vague suggestion of vitality, as if the daily regular pulse of civilization still beat, albeit languidly, in that remote extremity. There was anticipation and accomplishment twice a day; and as Key and Collinson rode up to the express-office, the express-wagon was standing before the door ready to start to meet the stagecoach at the cross-roads three miles away. This again seemed a special providence to Key. He had a brief official communication with Skinner as registrar, and duly recorded his claim; he had a hasty and confidential aside with Skinner as general storekeeper, and such was the unconscious magnetism developed by this embryo millionaire that Skinner extended the necessary credit to Collinson on Key's word alone. That done, he rejoined Collinson in high spirits with the news, adding cheerfully, "And I dare say, if you want any further advances Skinner will give them to you on Parker's draft."

"You mean that bit o' paper that chap left," said Collinson gravely.

"Yes."

"I tore it up."

"You tore it up?" ejaculated Key.

"You hear me? Yes!" said Collinson.

Key stared at him. Surely it was again providential that he had not intrusted his secret to this utterly ignorant and prejudiced man! The slight twinges of conscience that his lie about the slippers had caused him disappeared at once. He could not have trusted him even in that; it would have been like this stupid fanatic to have prevented Key's preemption of that claim, until he, Collinson, had satisfied himself of the whereabouts of the missing proprietor. Was he quite sure that Collinson would not revisit the spot when he had gone? But he was ready for the emergency.

He had intended to leave his horse with Skinner as security for Collinson's provisions, but Skinner's liberality had made this unnecessary, and he now offered it to Collinson to use and keep for him until called for. This would enable his companion to "pack" his goods on the mule, and oblige him to return to the mill by the wagon-road and "outside trail," as more commodious for the two animals.

"Ye ain't afeared o' the road agents?" suggested a bystander; "they just swarm on galloper's Ridge, and they 'held up' the down stage only last week."

"They're not so lively since the deputy-sheriff's got a new idea about them, and has been lying low in the brush near Bald Top," returned Skinner. "Anyhow, they don't stop teams nor 'packs' unless there's a chance of their getting some fancy horseflesh by it; and I reckon thar ain't much to tempt them thar," he added, with a satirical side glance at his customer's cattle. But Key was already standing in the express-wagon, giving a farewell shake to his patient companion's hand, and this ingenuous pleasantry passed unnoticed. Nevertheless, as the express-wagon rolled away, his active fancy began to consider this new danger that might threaten the hidden wealth of his claim. But he reflected that for a time, at least, only the crude ore would be taken out and shipped to Marysville in a shape that offered no profit to the highwaymen. Had it been a gold mine!—but here again was the interposition of Providence!

A week later Preble Key returned to Skinner's with a

foreman and ten men, and an unlimited credit to draw upon at Marysville! Expeditions of this kind created no surprise at Skinner's. Parties had before this entered the wilderness gayly, none knew where or what for; the sedate and silent woods had kept their secret while there; they had evaporated, none knew when or where—often, alas! with an unpaid account at Skinner's. Consequently, there was nothing in Key's party to challenge curiosity. In another week a rambling, one-storied shed of pine logs occupied the site of the mysterious ruins, and contained the party; in two weeks excavations had been made, and the whole face of the outcrop was exposed; in three weeks every vestige of former tenancy which the fire had not consumed was trampled out by the alien feet of these toilers of the "Sylvan Silver Hollow Company." None of Key's former companions would have recognized the hollow in its blackened leveling and rocky foundation; even Collinson would not have remembered this stripped and splintered rock, with its heaps of fresh debris, as the place where he had overtaken Key. And Key himself had forgotten, in his triumph, everything but the chance experiment that had led to his success.

Perhaps it was well, therefore, that one night, when the darkness had mercifully fallen upon this scene of sylvan desolation, and its still more incongruous and unsavory human restoration, and the low murmur of the pines occasionally swelled up from the unscathed mountain-side, a loud shout and the trampling of horses' feet awoke the dwellers in the shanty. Springing to their feet, they hurriedly seized their weapons and rushed out, only to be confronted by a dark, motionless ring of horsemen, two flaming torches of pine knots, and a low but distinct voice of authority. In their excitement, half-awakened suspicion, and confusion, they were affected by its note of calm preparation and conscious power.

"Drop those guns—hold up your hands! We've got every man of you covered."

Key was no coward; the men, though flustered, were not cravens: but they obeyed. "Trot out your leader! Let him stand out there, clear, beside that torch!"

One of the gleaming pine knots disengaged itself from the dark circle and moved to the centre, as Preble Key, cool and confident, stepped beside it.

"That will do," said the immutable voice. "Now, we want Jack Riggs, Sydney Jack, French Pete, and One-eyed Charley."

A vivid reminiscence of the former night scene in the hollow —of his own and his companions voices raised in the darkness—flashed across Key. With an instinctive premonition that this invasion had something to do with the former tenant, he said calmly:—

"Who wants them?"

"The State of California," said the voice.

"The State of California must look further," returned Key in his old pleasant voice; "there are no such names among my party."

"Who are you?"

"The manager of the 'Sylvan Silver Hollow Company,' and these are my workmen.

There was a hurried movement, and the sound of whispering in the hitherto dark and silent circle, and then the voice rose again:

"You have the papers to prove that?"

"Yes, in the cabin. And you?"

"I've a warrant to the sheriff of Sierra."

There was a pause, and the voice went on less confidently:—

"How long have you been here?"

"Three weeks. I came here the day of the fire and took up this claim."

"There was no other house here?"

"There were ruins,—you can see them still. It may have been a burnt-up cabin."

The voice disengaged itself from the vague background and came slowly forwards:—

"It was a den of thieves. It was the hiding-place of Jack Riggs and his gang of road agents. I've been hunting this spot for three weeks. And now the whole thing's up!"

There was a laugh from Key's men, but it was checked as the owner of the voice slowly ranged up beside the burning torch and they saw his face. It was dark and set with the defeat of a brave man.

"Won't you come in and take something?" said Key kindly.

"No. It's enough fool work for me to have routed ye out already. But I suppose it's all in my d—d day's work!

Good-night! Forward there! Get!"

The two torches danced forwards, with the trailing off of vague shadows in dim procession; there was a clatter over the rocks and they were gone. Then, as Preble Key gazed after them, he felt that with them had passed the only shadow that lay upon his great fortune; and with the last tenant of the hollow a proscribed outlaw and fugitive, he was henceforth forever safe in his claim and his discovery. And yet, oddly enough, at that moment, as he turned away, for the first time in three weeks there passed before his fancy with a stirring of reproach a vision of the face that he had seen at the window.

CHAPTER III

Of the great discovery in Sylvan Silver Hollow it would seem that Collinson as yet knew nothing. In spite of Key's fears that he might stray there on his return from Skinner's, he did not, nor did he afterwards revisit the locality. Neither the news of the registry of the claim nor the arrival of Key's workmen ever reached him. The few travelers who passed his mill came from the valley to cross the Divide on their way to Skinner's, and returned by the longer but easier detour of the stage-road over Galloper's Ridge. He had no chance to participate in the prosperity that flowed from the opening of the mine, which plentifully besprinkled Skinner's settlement; he was too far away to profit even by the chance custom of Key's Sabbath wandering workmen. His isolation from civilization (for those who came to him from the valley were rude Western emigrants like himself) remained undisturbed. The return of the prospecting party to his humble hospitality that night had been an exceptional case; in his characteristic simplicity he did not dream that it was because they had nowhere else to go in their penniless condition. It was an incident to be pleasantly remembered, but whose nonrecurrence did not disturb his infinite patience. His pork barrel and flour sack had been replenished for other travelers; his own wants were few.

It was a day or two after the midnight visit of the sheriff to

Silver Hollow that Key galloped down the steep grade to Collinson's. He was amused, albeit, in his new importance, a little aggrieved also, to find that Collinson had as usual confounded his descent with that of the generally detached boulder, and that he was obliged to add his voice to the general uproar. This brought Collinson to his door.

"I've had your hoss hobbled out among the chickweed and clover in the green pasture back o' the mill, and he's picked up that much that he's lookin' fat and sassy," he said quietly, beginning to mechanically unstrap Key's bridle, even while his guest was in the act of dismounting. "His back's quite healed up."

Key could not restrain a shrug of impatience. It was three weeks since they had met,—three weeks crammed with excitement, energy, achievement, and fortune to Key; and yet this place and this man were as stupidly unchanged as when he had left them. A momentary fancy that this was the reality, that he himself was only awakening from some delusive dream, came over him. But Collinson's next words were practical.

"I reckoned that maybe you'd write from Marysville to Skinner to send for the hoss, and forward him to ye, for I never kalkilated you'd come back."

It was quite plain from this that Collinson had heard nothing. But it was also awkward, as Key would now have to tell the whole story, and reveal the fact that he had been really experimenting when Collinson overtook him in the hollow. He evaded this by post-dating his discovery of the richness of the ore until he had reached Marysville. But he found some difficulty in recounting his good fortune: he was naturally no boaster, he had no desire to impress Collinson with his penetration, nor the undaunted energy he had displayed in getting up his company and opening the mine, so that he was actually embarrassed by his own understatement; and under the grave, patient eyes of his companion, told his story at best lamely. Collinson's face betrayed neither profound interest nor the slightest resentment. When Key had ended his awkward recital, Collinson said slowly:—

"Then Uncle Dick and that other Parker feller ain't got no show in this yer find."

"No," said Key quickly. "Don't you remember we broke up our partnership that morning and went off our own ways. You don't suppose," he added with a forced half-laugh, "that if Uncle Dick or Parker had struck a lead after they left me, they'd have put me in it?"

"Wouldn't they?" asked Collinson gravely.

"Of course not." He laughed a little more naturally, but presently added, with an uneasy smile, "What makes you think they would?"

"Nuthin'!" said Collinson promptly.

Nevertheless, when they were seated before the fire, with glasses in their hands, Collinson returned patiently to the subject:

"You wuz saying they went their way, and you went yours. But your way was back on the old way that you'd all gone together."

But Key felt himself on firmer ground here, and answered deliberately and truthfully, "Yes, but I only went back to the hollow to satisfy myself if there really was any house there, and if there was, to warn the occupants of the approaching fire."

"And there was a house there," said Collinson thoughtfully.

"Only the ruins." He stopped and flushed quickly, for he remembered that he had denied its existence at their former meeting. "That is," he went on hurriedly, "I found out from the sheriff, you know, that there had been a house there. But," he added, reverting to his stronger position, "my going back there was an accident, and my picking up the outcrop was an accident, and had no more to do with our partnership prospecting than you had. In fact," he said, with a reassuring laugh, "you'd have had a better right to share in my claim, coming there as you did at that moment, than they. Why, if I'd have known what the thing was worth, I might have put you in—only it wanted capital and some experience." He was glad that he had pitched upon that excuse (it had only just occurred to him), and glanced affably at Collinson. But that gentleman said soberly:—

"No, you wouldn't nuther."

"Why not?" said Key half angrily.

Collinson paused. After a moment he said, "'Cos I wouldn't hev took anything outer thet place."

Key felt relieved. From what he knew of Collinson's vagaries he believed him. He was wise in not admitting him to his confidences at the beginning; he might have thought it his duty to tell others.

"I'm not so particular," he returned laughingly, "but the silver in that hole was never touched, nor I dare say even imagined by mortal man before. However, there is something else

Bret Harte

about the hollow that I want to tell you. You remember the slipper that you picked up?"

"Yes."

"Well, I lied to you about that; I never dropped it. On the contrary, I had picked up the mate of it very near where you found yours, and I wanted to know to whom it belonged. For I don't mind telling you now, Collinson, that I believe there WAS a woman in that house, and the same woman whose face I saw at the window. You remember how the boys joked me about it—well, perhaps I didn't care that you should laugh at me too, but I've had a sore conscience over my lie, for I remembered that you seemed to have some interest in the matter too, and I thought that maybe I might have thrown you off the scent. It seemed to me that if you had any idea who it was, we might now talk the matter over and compare notes. I think you said—at least, I gathered the idea from a remark of yours," he added hastily, as he remembered that the suggestion was his own, and a satirical one—"that it reminded you of your wife's slipper. Of course, as your wife is dead, that would offer no clue, and can only be a chance resemblance, unless"—He stopped.

"Have you got 'em yet?"

"Yes, both." He took them from the pocket of his riding-jacket.

As Collinson received them, his face took upon itself an even graver expression. "It's mighty cur'ous," he said reflectively, "but looking at the two of 'em the likeness is more fetchin'. Ye see, my wife had a STRAIGHT foot, and never wore reg'lar rights and lefts like other women, but kinder changed about; ye see, these shoes is reg'lar rights and lefts, but never was worn as sich!"

"There may be other women as peculiar," suggested Key.

"There MUST be," said Collinson quietly.

For an instant Key was touched with the manly security of the reply, for, remembering Uncle Dick's scandal, it had occurred to him that the unknown tenant of the robbers' den might be Collinson's wife. He was glad to be relieved on that point, and went on more confidently:—

"So, you see, this woman was undoubtedly in that house on the night of the fire. She escaped, and in a mighty hurry too, for she had not time to change her slippers for shoes; she escaped on horseback, for that is how she lost them. Now what was she doing there with those rascals, for the face I saw looked as innocent as a saint's."

"Seemed to ye sort o' contrairy, jist as I reckoned my wife's foot would have looked in a slipper that you said was GIV to ye," suggested Collinson pointedly, but with no implication of reproach in his voice.

"Yes," said Key impatiently.

"I've read yarns afore now about them Eyetalian brigands stealin' women," said Collinson reflectively, "but that ain't California road-agent style. Great Scott! if one even so much as spoke to a woman, they'd have been wiped outer the State long ago. No! the woman as WAS there came there to STAY!"

As Key's face did not seem to express either assent or satisfaction at this last statement, Collinson, after a glance at it, went on with a somewhat gentler gravity: "I see wot's troublin' YOU, Mr. Key; you've bin thinkin' that mebbe that poor woman might hev bin the better for a bit o' that fortin' that you discovered under the very spot where them slippers of hers had often trod. You're thinkin' that mebbe it might hev turned her and those men from their evil ways."

Mr. Key had been thinking nothing of the kind, but for some obscure reason the skeptical jeer that had risen to his lips remained unsaid. He rose impatiently. "Well, there seems to be no chance of discovering anything now; the house is burnt, the gang dispersed, and she has probably gone with them." He paused, and then laid three or four large gold pieces on the table. "It's for that old bill of our party, Collinson," he said. "I'll settle and collect from each. Some time when you come over to the mine, and I hope you'll give us a call, you can bring the horse. Meanwhile you can use him; you'll find he's a little quicker than the mule. How is business?" he added, with a perfunctory glance around the vacant room and dusty bar.

"Thar ain't much passin' this way," said Collinson with equal carelessness, as he gathered up the money, "'cept those boys from the valley, and they're most always strapped when they come here."

Key smiled as he observed that Collinson offered him no receipt, and, moreover, as he remembered that he had only Collinson's word for the destruction of Parker's draft. But he merely glanced at his unconscious host, and said nothing. After a pause he returned in a lighter tone: "I suppose you are rather out of the world here. Indeed, I had an idea at first of buying out your mill, Collinson, and putting in steam power to get out timber for our new buildings, but you see you are so far away from the wagon-road, that we couldn't haul the timber away. That was the trouble, or I'd have made you a fair offer."

"I don't reckon to ever sell the mill," said Collinson simply.

Then observing the look of suspicion in his companion's face, he added gravely, "You see, I rigged up the whole thing when I expected my wife out from the States, and I calkilate to keep it in memory of her."

Key slightly lifted his brows. "But you never told us, by the way, HOW you ever came to put up a mill here with such an uncertain water-supply."

"It wasn't onsartin when I came here, Mr. Key; it was a full-fed stream straight from them snow peaks. It was the earthquake did it."

"The earthquake!" repeated Key.

"Yes. Ef the earthquake kin heave up that silver-bearing rock that you told us about the first day you kem here, and that you found t'other day, it could play roots with a mere mill-stream, I reckon."

"But the convulsion I spoke of happened ages on ages ago, when this whole mountain range was being fashioned," said Key with a laugh.

"Well, this yer earthquake was ten years ago, just after I came. I reckon I oughter remember it. It was a queer sort o' day in the fall, dry and hot as if thar might hev bin a fire in the woods, only thar wasn't no wind. Not a breath of air anywhar. The leaves of them alders hung straight as a plumb-line. Except for that thar stream and that thar wheel, nuthin' moved. Thar wasn't a bird on the wing over that canyon; thar wasn't a squirrel skirmishin' in the hull wood; even the lizards in the rocks stiffened like stone Chinese idols. It kept gettin' quieter and quieter, ontil I walked out on that ledge and felt as if I'd have to give a yell just to hear my own voice. Thar was a thin veil over everything, and betwixt and between everything, and the sun was rooted in the middle of it as if it couldn't move neither. Everythin' seemed to be waitin', waitin', waitin'. Then all of a suddin suthin' seemed to give somewhar! Suthin' fetched away with a queer sort of rumblin', as if the peg had slipped outer creation. I looked up and kalkilated to see half a dozen of them boulders come, lickity switch, down the grade. But, darn my skin, if one of 'em stirred! and yet while I was looking, the whole face o' that bluff bowed over softly, as if saying 'Good-by,' and got clean away somewhar before I knowed it. Why, you see that pile agin the side o' the canyon! Well, a thousand feet under that there's trees, three hundred feet high, still upright and standin'. You know how them pines over on that far mountain-side always seem to be climbin' up, up, up, over each other's heads to the very top? Well, Mr. Key, I SAW 'EM climbin'! And when I pulled myself together and got back to the mill, everything was quiet; and, by G—d, so was the mill-wheel, and there wasn't two inches of water in the river!"

"And what did you think of it?" said Key, interested in spite of his impatience.

"I thought, Mr. Key—No! I mustn't say I thought, for I knowed it. I knowed that suthin' had happened to my wife!"

Key did not smile, but even felt a faint superstitious thrill as he gazed at him. After a pause Collinson resumed: "I heard a month after that she had died about that time o' yaller fever in Texas with the party she was comin' with. Her folks wrote that they died like flies, and wuz all buried together, unbeknownst and promiscuous, and thar wasn't no remains. She slipped away from me like that bluff over that canyon, and that was the end of it."

"But she might have escaped," said Key quickly, forgetting

himself in his eagerness.

But Collinson only shook his head. "Then she'd have been here," he said gravely.

Key moved towards the door still abstractedly, held out his hand, shook that of his companion warmly, and then, saddling his horse himself, departed. A sense of disappointment—in which a vague dissatisfaction with himself was mingled—was all that had come of his interview. He took himself severely to task for following his romantic quest so far. It was unworthy of the president of the Sylvan Silver Hollow Company, and he was not quite sure but that his confidences with Collinson might have imperiled even the interests of the company. To atone for this momentary aberration, and correct his dismal fancies, he resolved to attend to some business at Skinner's before returning, and branched off on a long detour that would intersect the traveled stage-road. But here a singular incident overtook him. As he wheeled into the turnpike, he heard the trampling hoof-beats and jingling harness of the oncoming coach behind him. He had barely time to draw up against the bank before the six galloping horses and swinging vehicle swept heavily by. He had a quick impression of the heat and steam of sweating horse-hide, the reek of varnish and leather, and the momentary vision of a female face silhouetted against the glass window of the coach! But even in that flash of perception he recognized the profile that he had seen at the window of the mysterious hut!

He halted for an instant dazed and bewildered in the dust of the departing wheels. Then, as the bulk of the vehicle reappeared, already narrowing in the distance, without a second thought he dashed after it. His disappointment, his self-criticism, his practical resolutions were forgotten. He had but one idea now—the vision was providential! The clue to the mystery was before him—he MUST follow it!

Yet he had sense enough to realize that the coach would not stop to take up a passenger between stations, and that the next station was the one three miles below Skinner's. It would not be difficult to reach this by a cut-off in time, and although the vehicle had appeared to be crowded, he could no doubt obtain a seat on top.

His eager curiosity, however, led him to put spurs to his horse, and range up alongside of the coach as if passing it, while he examined the stranger more closely. Her face was bent listlessly over a book; there was unmistakably the same profile that he had seen, but the full face was different in outline and expression. A strange sense of disappointment that was almost a revulsion of feeling came over him; he lingered, he glanced again; she was certainly a very pretty woman: there was the beautifully rounded chin, the short straight nose, and delicately curved upper lip, that he had seen in the profile,—and yet—yet it was not the same face he had dreamt of. With an odd, provoking sense of disillusion, he swept ahead of the coach, and again slackened his speed to let it pass. This time the fair unknown raised her long lashes and gazed suddenly at this persistent horseman at her side, and an odd expression, it seemed to him almost a glance of recognition and expectation, came into her dark, languid eyes. The pupils concentrated upon him with a singular significance, that was almost, he even thought, a reply to his glance, and yet it was as utterly unintelligible. A moment later, however, it was explained. He had fallen slightly behind in a new confusion of hesitation, wonder, and embarrassment, when from a wooded trail to the right, another horseman suddenly swept into the road before him. He was a powerfully built man, mounted on a thoroughbred horse of a quality far superior to the ordinary roadster. Without looking at Key he easily ranged up beside the coach as if to pass it, but Key, with a sudden resolution, put spurs to his own horse and ranged also abreast of him, in time to see his fair unknown start at the apparition of this second horseman and unmistakably convey some signal to him,—a signal that to Key's fancy now betrayed some warning of himself. He was the more convinced as the stranger, after continuing a few paces ahead of the coach, allowed it to pass him at a curve of the road, and slackened his pace to permit Key to do the same. Instinctively conscious that the stranger's object was to scrutinize or identify him, he determined to take the initiative, and fixed his eyes upon him as they approached. But the stranger, who wore a loose brown linen duster over clothes that appeared to be superior in fashion and material, also had part of his face and head draped by a white silk handkerchief worn under his hat, ostensibly to keep the sun and dust from his head and neck,—and had the advantage of him. He only caught the flash of a pair of steel-gray eyes, as the newcomer, apparently having satisfied himself, gave rein to his spirited steed and easily repassed the coach, disappearing in a cloud of dust before it. But Key had by this time reached the "cut-off," which the stranger, if he intended to follow the coach, either disdained or was ignorant of, and he urged his horse to its utmost speed. Even with the stranger's advantages it would be a close race to the station.

Nevertheless, as he dashed on, he was by no means insensible to the somewhat quixotic nature of his undertaking. If he was right in his suspicion that a signal had been given by the lady to the stranger, it was exceedingly probable that he had discovered not only the fair inmate of the robbers' den, but one of the gang itself, or at least a confederate and ally. Yet far from deterring him, in that ingenious sophistry with which he was apt to treat his romance, he now looked upon his adventure as a practical pursuit in the interests of law and justice. It was true that it was said that the band of road agents had been dispersed; it was a fact that there had been no spoliation of coach or teams for three weeks; but none of the depredators had ever been caught, and their booty, which was considerable, was known to be still intact. It was to the interest of the mine, his partners, and his workmen that this clue to a danger which threatened the locality should be followed to the end. As to the lady, in spite of the disappointment that still rankled in his breast, he could be magnanimous! She might be the paramour of the strange horseman, she might be only escaping from some hateful companionship by his aid. And yet one thing puzzled him: she was evidently not acquainted with the personality of the active gang, for she had, without doubt, at first mistaken HIM for one of them, and after recognizing her real accomplice had communicated her mistake to him.

It was a great relief to him when the rough and tangled "cut-off" at last broadened and lightened into the turnpike road again, and he beheld, scarcely a quarter of a mile before him, the dust cloud that overhung the coach as it drew up at the lonely wayside station. He was in time, for he knew that the horses were changed there; but a sudden fear that the fair unknown might alight, or take some other conveyance, made him still spur his jaded steed forward. As he neared the station he glanced eagerly around for the other horseman, but he was nowhere to be seen. He had evidently either abandoned the chase or ridden ahead.

It seemed equally a part of what he believed was a providential intercession, that on arriving at the station he found there was a vacant seat inside the coach. It was diagonally opposite that occupied by the lady, and he was thus enabled to study her face as it was bent over her book, whose pages, however, she scarcely turned. After her first casual glance of curiosity at the new passenger, she seemed to take no more notice of him, and Key began to wonder if he had not mistaken her previous interrogating look. Nor was it his only disturbing query; he was conscious of the same disappointment now that he could examine her face more attentively, as in his first cursory glance. She was certainly handsome; if there was no longer the freshness of youth, there was still the indefinable charm of the woman of thirty, and with it the delicate curves of matured muliebrity and repose. There were lines, particularly around the mouth and fringed eyelids, that were deepened as by pain; and the chin, even in its rounded fullness, had the angle of determination. From what was visible, below the brown linen duster that she wore, she appeared to be tastefully although not richly dressed.

As the coach at last drove away from the station, a grizzled, farmer-looking man seated beside her uttered a sigh of relief, so palpable as to attract the general attention. Turning to his fair neighbor with a smile of uncouth but good-humored apology, he said in explanation:—

"You'll excuse me, miss! I don't know ezactly how YOU'RE feelin',—for judging from your looks and gin'ral gait, you're a stranger in these parts,—but ez for ME, I don't mind sayin' that I never feel ezactly safe from these yer road agents and stage robbers ontil arter we pass Skinner's station. All along thet Galloper's Ridge it's jest tech and go like; the woods is swarmin' with 'em. But once past Skinner's, you're all right. They never dare go below that. So ef you don't mind, miss, for it's bein' in your presence, I'll jest pull off my butes and ease my feet for a spell."

Neither the inconsequence of this singular request, nor the smile it evoked on the faces of the other passengers, seemed to disturb the lady's abstraction. Scarcely lifting her eyes from her book, she bowed a grave assent.

"You see, miss," he continued, " and you gents," he added,

taking the whole coach into his confidence, "I've got over forty ounces of clean gold dust in them butes, between the upper and lower sole,—and it's mighty tight packing for my feet. Ye kin heft it," he said, as he removed one boot and held it up before them. "I put the dust there for safety— kalkilatin' that while these road gentry allus goes for a man's pockets and his body belt, they never thinks of his butes, or haven't time to go through 'em." He looked around him with a smile of self-satisfaction.

The murmur of admiring comment was, however, broken by a burly-bearded miner who sat in the middle seat. "Thet's pretty fair, as far as it goes," he said smilingly, "but I reckon it wouldn't go far ef you started to run. I've got a simpler game than that, gentlemen, and ez we're all friends here, and the danger's over, I don't mind tellin' ye. The first thing these yer road agents do, after they've covered the driver with their shot guns, is to make the passengers get out and hold up their hands. That, ma'am,"—explanatorily to the lady, who betrayed only a languid interest,—"is to keep 'em from drawing their revolvers. A revolver is the last thing a road agent wants, either in a man's hand or in his holster. So I sez to myself, 'Ef a six-shooter ain't of no account, wet's the use of carryin' it?' So I just put my shooting-iron in my valise when I travel, and fill my holster with my gold dust, so! It's a deuced sight heavier than a revolver, but they don't feel its weight, and don't keer to come nigh it. And I've been 'held up' twice on t'other side of the Divide this year, and I passed free every time!"

The applause that followed this revelation and the exhibition of the holster not only threw the farmer's exploits into the shade, but seemed to excite an emulation among the passengers. Other methods of securing their property were freely discussed; but the excitement culminated in the leaning forward of a passenger who had, up to that moment, maintained a reserve almost equal to the fair unknown. His dress and general appearance were those of a professional man; his voice and manner corroborated the presumption.

"I don't think, gentlemen," he began with a pleasant smile, "that any man of us here would like to be called a coward; but in fighting with an enemy who never attacks, or even appears, except with a deliberately prepared advantage on his side, it is my opinion that a man is not only justified in avoiding an unequal encounter with him, but in circumventing by every means the object of his attack. You have all been frank in telling your methods. I will be equally so in telling mine, even if I have perhaps to confess to a little more than you have; for I have not only availed myself of a well-known rule of the robbers who infest these mountains, to exempt all women and children from their spoliation,—a rule which, of course, they perfectly understand gives them a sentimental consideration with all Californians,—but I have, I confess, also availed myself of the innocent kindness of one of that charming and justly exempted sex." He paused and bowed courteously to the fair unknown. "When I entered this coach I had with me a bulky parcel which was manifestly too large for my pockets, yet as evidently too small and too valuable to be intrusted to the ordinary luggage. Seeing my difficulty, our charming companion opposite, out of the very kindness and innocence of her heart, offered to make a place for it in her satchel, which was not full. I accepted the offer joyfully. When I state to you, gentlemen, that that package contained valuable government bonds to a considerable amount, I do so, not to claim your praise for any originality of my own, but to make this public avowal to our fair fellow passenger for securing to me this most perfect security and immunity from the road agent that has been yet recorded."

With his eyes riveted on the lady's face, Key saw a faint color rise to her otherwise impassive face, which might have been called out by the enthusiastic praise that followed the lawyer's confession. But he was painfully conscious of what now seemed to him a monstrous situation! Here was, he believed, the actual accomplice of the road agents calmly receiving the complacent and puerile confessions of the men who were seeking to outwit them. Could he, in ordinary justice to them, to himself, or the mission he conceived he was pursuing, refrain from exposing her, or warning them privately? But was he certain? Was a vague remembrance of a profile momentarily seen—and, as he must even now admit, inconsistent with the full face he was gazing at— sufficient for such an accusation? More than that, was the protection she had apparently afforded the lawyer consistent with the function of an accomplice!

"Then if the danger's over," said the lady gently, reaching down to draw her satchel from under the seat, "I suppose I may return it to you."

"By no means! Don't trouble yourself! Pray allow me to still remain your debtor,—at least as far as the next station," said the lawyer gallantly.

The lady uttered a languid sigh, sank back in her seat, and calmly settled herself to the perusal of her book. Key felt his cheeks beginning to burn with the embarrassment and shame of his evident misconception. And here he was on his way to Marysville, to follow a woman for whom he felt he no longer cared, and for whose pursuit he had no longer the excuse of justice.

"Then I understand that you have twice seen these road agents," said the professional man, turning to the miner. "Of course, you could be able to identify them?"

"Nary a man! You see they're all masked, and only one of

'em ever speaks."

"The leader or chief?"

"No, the orator."

"The orator?" repeated the professional man in amazement.

"Well, you see, I call him the orator, for he's mighty glib with his tongue, and reels off all he has to say like as if he had it by heart. He's mighty rough on you, too, sometimes, for all his high-toned style. Ef he thinks a man is hidin' anything he jest scalps him with his tongue, and blamed if I don't think he likes the chance of doin' it. He's got a regular set speech, and he's bound to go through it all, even if he makes everything wait, and runs the risk of capture. Yet he ain't the chief,—and even I've heard folks say ain't got any responsibility if he is took, for he don't tech anybody or anybody's money, and couldn't be prosecuted. I reckon he's some sort of a broken-down lawyer—d'ye see?"

"Not much of a lawyer, I imagine," said the professional man, smiling, "for he'll find himself quite mistaken as to his share of responsibility. But it's a rather clever way of concealing the identity of the real leader."

"It's the smartest gang that was ever started in the Sierras. They fooled the sheriff of Sierra the other day. They gave him a sort of idea that they had a kind of hidin'-place in the woods whar they met and kept their booty, and, by jinks! he goes down thar with his hull posse,—just spilin' for a fight,—and only lights upon a gang of innocent greenhorns, who were boring for silver on the very spot where he allowed the robbers had their den! He ain't held up his head since."

Bret Harte

Key cast a quick glance at the lady to see the effect of this revelation. But her face—if the same profile he had seen at the window—betrayed neither concern nor curiosity. He let his eyes drop to the smart boot that peeped from below her gown, and the thought of his trying to identify it with the slipper he had picked up seemed to him as ridiculous as his other misconceptions. He sank back gloomily in his seat; by degrees the fatigue and excitement of the day began to mercifully benumb his senses; twilight had fallen and the talk had ceased. The lady had allowed her book to drop in her lap as the darkness gathered, and had closed her eyes; he closed his own, and slipped away presently into a dream, in which he saw the profile again as he had seen it in the darkness of the hollow, only that this time it changed to a full face, unlike the lady's or any one he had ever seen. Then the window seemed to open with a rattle, and he again felt the cool odors of the forest; but he awoke to find that the lady had only opened her window for a breath of fresh air. It was nearly eight o' clock; it would be an hour yet before the coach stopped at the next station for supper; the passengers were drowsily nodding; he closed his eyes and fell into a deeper sleep, from which he awoke with a start.

The coach had stopped!

CHAPTER IV

"It can't be Three Pines yet," said a passenger's voice, in which the laziness of sleep still lingered, "or else we've snoozed over five mile. I don't see no lights; wot are we stoppin' for?" The other passengers struggled to an upright position. One nearest the window opened it; its place was instantly occupied by the double muzzle of a shot-gun! No one moved. In the awestricken silence the voice of the driver rose in drawling protestation.

"It ain't no business o' mine, but it sorter strikes me that you chaps are a-playin' it just a little too fine this time! It ain't three miles from Three Pine Station and forty men. Of course, that's your lookout,—not mine!"

The audacity of the thing had evidently struck even the usually taciturn and phlegmatic driver into his first expostulation on record.

"Your thoughtful consideration does you great credit," said a voice from the darkness, "and shall be properly presented to our manager; but at the same time we wish it understood that we do not hesitate to take any risks in strict attention to our business and our clients. In the mean time you will expedite matters, and give your passengers a chance to get an early tea at Three Pines, by handing down that treasure-box and mail-pouch. Be careful in handling that blunderbuss you keep beside it; the last time it unfortunately went off, and I regret to say slightly wounded one of your passengers. Accidents of this kind, interfering, as they do, with the harmony and pleasure of our chance meetings, cannot be too highly deplored."

"By gosh!" ejaculated an outside passenger in an audible whisper.

"Thank you, sir," said the voice quietly; "but as I overlooked you, I will trouble you now to descend with the others."

The voice moved nearer; and, by the light of a flaming bull's-eye cast upon the coach, it could be seen to come from a stout, medium-sized man with a black mask, which, however, showed half of a smooth, beardless face, and an affable yet satirical mouth. The speaker cleared his throat with the slight preparatory cough of the practiced orator, and, approaching the window, to Key's intense surprise, actually began in the identical professional and rhetorical style previously indicated by the miner.

"Circumstances over which we have no control, gentlemen, compel us to oblige you to alight, stand in a row on one side, and hold up your hands. You will find the attitude not unpleasant after your cramped position in the coach, while the change from its confined air to the wholesome night-breeze of the Sierras cannot but prove salutary and refreshing. It will also enable us to relieve you of such so-called valuables and treasures in the way of gold dust and coin, which I regret to say too often are misapplied in careless hands, and which the teachings of the highest morality distinctly denominate as the root of all evil! I need not inform you, gentlemen, as business men, that promptitude and celerity of compliance will insure dispatch, and shorten an interview which has been sometimes needlessly, and, I regret to say, painfully protracted."

He drew back deliberately with the same monotonous precision of habit, and disclosed the muzzles of his confederates' weapons still leveled at the passengers. In spite of their astonishment, indignation, and discomfiture, his practiced effrontery and deliberate display appeared in some way to touch their humorous sense, and one or two smiled hysterically, as they rose and hesitatingly filed out of the vehicle. It is possible, however, that the leveled shot-guns contributed more or less directly to this result.

Two masks began to search the passengers under the combined focus of the bull's-eyes, the shining gun-barrels, and a running but still carefully prepared commentary from the spokesman. "It is to be regretted that business men, instead of intrusting their property to the custody of the regularly constituted express agent, still continue to secrete it on their persons; a custom that, without enhancing its security, is not only an injustice to the express company, but a great detriment to dispatch. We also wish to point out that while we do not as a rule interfere with the possession of articles of ordinary personal use or adornment, such as simple jewelry or watches, we reserve our right to restrict by confiscation the vulgarity and unmanliness of diamonds and enormous fob chains."

The act of spoliation was apparently complete, yet it was evident that the orator was restraining himself for a more effective climax. Clearing his throat again and stepping before the impatient but still mystified file of passengers, he reviewed them gravely. Then in a perfectly pitched tone of mingled pain and apology, he said slowly:—

"It would seem that, from no wish of our own, we are

obliged on this present occasion to suspend one or two of our usual rules. We are not in the habit of interfering with the wearing apparel of our esteemed clients; but in the interests of ordinary humanity we are obliged to remove the boots of the gentleman on the extreme left, which evidently give him great pain and impede his locomotion. We also seldom deviate from our rule of obliging our clients to hold up their hands during this examination; but we gladly make an exception in favor of the gentleman next to him, and permit him to hand us the altogether too heavily weighted holster which presses upon his hip. Gentlemen," said the orator, slightly raising his voice, with a deprecating gesture, "you need not be alarmed! The indignant movement of our friend, just now, was not to draw his revolver,—for it isn't there!" He paused while his companions speedily removed the farmer's boots and the miner's holster, and with a still more apologetic air approached the coach, where only the lady remained erect and rigid in her corner. "And now," he said with simulated hesitation, "we come to the last and to us the most painful suspension of our rules. On these very rare occasions, when we have been honored with the presence of the fair sex, it has been our invariable custom not only to leave them in the undisturbed possession of their property, but even of their privacy as well. It is with deep regret that on this occasion we are obliged to make an exception. For in the present instance, the lady, out of the gentleness of her heart and the politeness of her sex, has burdened herself not only with the weight but the responsibility of a package forced upon her by one of the passengers. We feel, and we believe, gentlemen, that most of you will agree with us, that so scandalous and unmanly an attempt to evade our rules and violate the sanctity of the lady's immunity will never be permitted. For your own sake, madam, we are compelled to ask you for the satchel under your seat. It will be returned to you when the package is removed."

"One moment," said the professional man indignantly, "there is a man here whom you have spared,—a man who lately joined us. Is that man," pointing to the astonished Key, "one of your confederates?"

"That man," returned the spokesman with a laugh, "is the owner of the Sylvan Hollow Mine. We have spared him because we owe him some consideration for having been turned out of his house at the dead of night while the sheriff of Sierra was seeking us." He stopped, and then in an entirely different voice, and in a totally changed manner, said roughly, "Tumble in there, all of you, quick! And you, sir" (to Key),—"I'd advise you to ride outside. Now, driver, raise so much as a rein or a whiplash until you hear the signal— and by God! you'll know what next." He stepped back, and seemed to be instantly swallowed up in the darkness; but the light of a solitary bull's-eye—the holder himself invisible— still showed the muzzles of the guns covering the driver. There was a momentary stir of voices within the closed coach, but an angry roar of "Silence!" from the darkness hushed it.

The moments crept slowly by; all now were breathless. Then a clear whistle rang from the distance, the light suddenly was extinguished, the leveled muzzles vanished with it, the driver's lash fell simultaneously on the backs of his horses, and the coach leaped forward.

The jolt nearly threw Key from the top, but a moment later it was still more difficult to keep his seat in the headlong fury of their progress. Again and again the lash descended upon the maddened horses, until the whole coach seemed to leap, bound, and swerve with every stroke. Cries of protest and even distress began to come from the interior, but the driver heeded it not. A window was suddenly let down; the voice of the professional man saying, "What's the matter? We're not followed. You are imperiling our lives by this speed," was answered only by, "Will some of ye throttle that d—d fool?" from the driver, and the renewed fall of the lash. The wayside trees appeared a solid plateau before them, opened, danced at their side, closed up again behind them,—but still they sped along. Rushing down grades with the speed of an avalanche, they ascended again without drawing rein, and as if by sheer momentum; for the heavy vehicle now seemed to have a diabolical energy of its own. It ground scattered rocks to powder with its crushing wheels, it swayed heavily on ticklish corners, recovering itself with the resistless forward propulsion of the straining teams, until the lights of Three Pine Station began to glitter through the trees. Then a succession of yells broke from the driver, so strong and dominant that they seemed to outstrip even the speed of the unabated cattle. Lesser lights were presently seen running to and fro, and on the outermost fringe of the settlement the stage pulled up before a crowd of wondering faces, and the driver spoke.

"We've been held up on the open road, by G—d, not THREE MILES from whar ye men are sittin' here yawpin'! If thar's a man among ye that hasn't got the soul of a skunk, he'll foller and close in upon 'em before they have a chance to get into the brush." Having thus relieved himself of his duty as an enforced noncombatant, and allowed all further responsibility to devolve upon his recreant fellow employees, he relapsed into his usual taciturnity, and drove a trifle less recklessly to the station, where he grimly set down his bruised and discomfited passengers. As Key mingled with them, he could not help perceiving that neither the late "orator's" explanation of his exemption from their fate, nor the driver's surly corroboration of his respectability, had pacified them. For a time this amused him, particularly as he could not help remembering that he first appeared to them beside the mysterious horseman who some one thought had been identified as one of the masks. But he was not a little piqued to find that the fair unknown appeared to participate in their feelings, and his first civility to her met with a chilling response. Even then, in the general disillusion of his romance regarding her, this would have been only a momentary annoyance; but it strangely revived all his previous suspicions, and set him to thinking. Was the singular sagacity displayed by the orator in his search purely intuitive? Could any one have disclosed to him the secret of the passengers' hoards? Was it possible for HER while sitting alone in the coach to have communicated with the band? Suddenly the remembrance flashed across him of her opening the window for fresh air! She could have easily then dropped some signal. If this were so, and she really was the culprit, it was quite natural for her own safety that she should encourage the passengers in the absurd suspicion of himself! His dying interest revived; a few moments ago he had half resolved to abandon his quest and turn back at Three Pines. Now he determined to follow her to the end. But he did not indulge in any further sophistry regarding his duty; yet, in a new sense of honor, he did not dream of retaliating upon her by communicating his suspicions to his fellow passengers. When the coach started again, he took his seat on the top, and remained there until they reached Jamestown in the early evening. Here a number of his despoiled companions were obliged to wait, to communicate with their friends. Happily, the exemption that had made them indignant enabled him to continue his journey with a full purse. But he was content with a modest surveillance of the lady from the top of the coach.

On arriving at Stockton this surveillance became less easy. It was the terminus of the stage-route, and the divergence of others by boat and rail. If he were lucky enough to discover which one the lady took, his presence now would be more marked, and might excite her suspicion. But here a circumstance, which he also believed to be providential, determined him. As the luggage was being removed from the top of the coach, he overheard the agent tell the expressman to check the "lady's" trunk to San Luis. Key was seized with an idea which seemed to solve the difficulty, although it involved a risk of losing the clue entirely. There were two routes to San Luis, one was by stage, and direct, though slower; the other by steamboat and rail, via San Francisco. If he took the boat, there was less danger of her discovering him, even if she chose the same conveyance; if she took the direct stage,—and he trusted to a woman's avoidance of the hurry of change and transshipment for that choice,—he would still arrive at San Luis, via San Francisco, an hour before her. He resolved to take the boat; a careful scrutiny from a stateroom window of the arriving passengers on the gangplank satisfied him that she had preferred the stage. There was still the chance that in losing sight of her she might escape him, but the risk seemed small. And a trifling circumstance had almost unconsciously influenced him— after his romantic and superstitious fashion—as to this final step.

He had been singularly moved when he heard that San Luis was the lady's probable destination. It did not seem to bear any relation to the mountain wilderness and the wild life she had just quitted; it was apparently the most antipathic, incongruous, and inconsistent refuge she could have taken. It offered no opportunity for the disposal of booty, or for communication with the gang. It was less secure than a crowded town. An old Spanish mission and monastery college in a sleepy pastoral plain,—it had even retained its old-world flavor amidst American improvements and social revolution. He knew it well. From the quaint college cloisters, where the only reposeful years of his adventurous youth had been spent, to the long Alameda, or double avenues of ancient trees, which connected it with the convent of Santa Luisa, and some of his youthful "devotions,"—it had been the nursery of his romance. He was amused at what seemed to be the irony of fate, in now linking it with this folly of his maturer manhood; and yet he was uneasily conscious of being more seriously affected by it. And it was with a greater anxiety than this adventure had ever yet cost him that he at last arrived at the San Jose hotel, and from a balcony corner awaited the coming of the coach. His heart beat rapidly as it approached. She was there! But at her side, as she descended from the coach, was the mysterious horseman of the Sierra road. Key could not mistake the well-built figure, whatever doubt there had been about the features, which had been so carefully concealed. With the astonishment of this rediscovery, there flashed across him again the fatefulness of the inspiration which had decided him not to go in the coach. His presence there would have no doubt warned the stranger, and so estopped this convincing denouement. It was quite possible that her companion, by relays of horses and the advantage of bridle cut-offs, could have easily followed the Three Pine coach and joined her at Stockton. But for what purpose? The lady's trunk, which had not been disturbed during the first part of the journey, and had been forwarded at Stockton untouched before Key's eyes, could not have contained booty to be disposed of in this forgotten old town.

The register of the hotel bore simply the name of "Mrs. Barker," of Stockton, but no record of her companion, who seemed to have disappeared as mysteriously as he came. That she occupied a sitting-room on the same floor as his own—in which she was apparently secluded during the rest of the day—was all he knew. Nobody else seemed to know her. Key felt an odd hesitation, that might have been the result of some vague fear of implicating her prematurely, in making any marked inquiry, or imperiling his secret by the bribed espionage of servants. Once when he was passing her door he heard the sounds of laughter,—albeit innocent and heart-free,—which seemed so inconsistent with the gravity of the situation and his own thoughts that he was strangely shocked. But he was still more disturbed by a later occurrence. In his watchfulness of the movements of his neighbor he had been equally careful of his own, and had not only refrained from registering his name, but had enjoined secrecy upon the landlord, whom he knew. Yet the next morning after his arrival, the porter not answering his bell promptly enough, he so far forgot himself as to walk to the staircase, which was near the lady's room, and call to the employee over the balustrade. As he was still leaning over the railing, the faint creak of a door, and a singular magnetic consciousness of being overlooked, caused him to turn slowly, but only in time to hear the rustle of a withdrawing skirt as the door was quickly closed. In an instant he felt the full force of his foolish heedlessness, but it was too late. Had the mysterious fugitive recognized him? Perhaps not; their eyes had not met, and his face had been turned away.

He varied his espionage by subterfuges, which his know-ledge of the old town made easy. He watched the door of the hotel, himself unseen, from the windows of a billiard saloon opposite, which he had frequented in former days. Yet he was surprised the same afternoon to see her, from his coigne of vantage, reentering the hotel, where he was sure he had left her a few moments ago. Had she gone out by some other exit,—or had she been disguised? But on entering his room that evening he was confounded by an incident that seemed to him as convincing of her identity as it was audacious. Lying on his pillow were a few dead leaves of an odorous mountain fern, known only to the Sierras. They were tied together by a narrow blue ribbon, and had evidently been intended to attract his attention. As he took them in his hand, the distinguishing subtle aroma of the little sylvan hollow in the hills came to him like a memory and a revelation! He summoned the chambermaid; she knew nothing of them, or indeed of any one who had entered his room. He walked cautiously into the hall; the lady's sitting-room door was open, the room was empty. "The occupant," said the chambermaid, "had left that afternoon." He held the proof of her identity in his hand, but she herself had vanished! That she had recognized him there was now no doubt: had she divined the real object of his quest, or had she accepted it as a mere sentimental gallantry at the moment when she knew it was hopeless, and she herself was perfectly safe from pursuit? In either event he had been duped. He did not know whether to be piqued, angry,—or relieved of his irresolute quest.

Nevertheless, he spent the rest of the twilight and the early evening in fruitlessly wandering through the one long thoroughfare of the town, until it merged into the bosky Alameda, or spacious grove, that connected it with Santa Luisa. By degrees his chagrin and disappointment were forgotten in the memories of the past, evoked by the familiar pathway. The moon was slowly riding overhead, and silvering the carriage-way between the straight ebony lines of trees, while the footpaths were diapered with black and white checkers. The faint tinkling of a tram-car bell in the distance apprised him of one of the few innovations of the past. The car was approaching him, overtook him, and was passing, with its faintly illuminated windows, when, glancing carelessly up, he beheld at one of them the profile of the face which he had just thought he had lost forever!

He stopped for an instant, not in indecision this time, but in a grim resolution to let no chance escape him now. The car was going slowly; it was easy to board it now, but again the tinkle of the bell indicated that it was stopping at the corner of a road beyond. He checked his pace,—a lady alighted,—it was she! She turned into the cross-street, darkened with the shadows of some low suburban tenement houses, and he boldly followed. He was fully determined to find out her secret, and even, if necessary, to accost her for that purpose. He was perfectly aware what he was doing, and all its risks and penalties; he knew the audacity of such an introduction, but he felt in his left-hand pocket for the sprig of fern which was an excuse for it; he knew the danger of following a possible confidante of desperadoes, but he felt in his right-hand pocket for the derringer that was equal to it. They were both there; he was ready.

He was nearing the convent and the oldest and most ruinous part of the town. He did not disguise from himself the gloomy significance of this; even in the old days the crumbling adobe buildings that abutted on the old garden wall of the convent were the haunts of lawless Mexicans and vagabond peons. As the roadway began to be rough and uneven, and the gaunt outlines of the sagging roofs of tiles stood out against the sky above the lurking shadows of ruined doorways, he was prepared for the worst. As the crumbling but still massive walls of the convent garden loomed ahead, the tall, graceful, black-gowned figure he was following presently turned into the shadow of the wall itself. He quickened his pace, lest it should again escape him. Suddenly it stopped, and remained motionless. He stopped, too. At the same moment it vanished!

He ran quickly forward to where it had stood, and found himself before a large iron gate, with a smaller one in the centre, that had just clanged to on its rusty hinges. He rubbed his eyes!—the place, the gate, the wall, were all strangely familiar! Then he stepped back into the roadway, and looked at it again. He was not mistaken.

He was standing before the porter's lodge of the Convent of the Sacred Heart.

CHAPTER V

The day following the great stagecoach robbery found the patient proprietor of Collinson's Mill calm and untroubled in his usual seclusion. The news that had thrilled the length and breadth of Galloper's Ridge had not touched the leafy banks of the dried-up river; the hue and cry had followed the stage-road, and no courier had deemed it worth his while to diverge as far as the rocky ridge which formed the only pathway to the mill. That day Collinson's solitude had been unbroken even by the haggard emigrant from the valley, with his old monotonous story of hardship and privation. The birds had flown nearer to the old mill, as if emboldened by the unwonted quiet. That morning there had been the half human imprint of a bear's foot in the ooze beside the mill-wheel; and coming home with his scant stock from the woodland pasture, he had found a golden squirrel—a beautiful, airy embodiment of the brown woods itself—calmly seated on his bar-counter, with a biscuit between its baby hands. He was full of his characteristic reveries and abstractions that afternoon; falling into them even at his wood-pile, leaning on his axe—so still that an emerald-throated lizard, who had slid upon the log, went to sleep under the forgotten stroke.

But at nightfall the wind arose,—at first as a distant murmur along the hillside, that died away before it reached the rocky

Bret Harte

ledge; then it rocked the tops of the tall redwoods behind the mill, but left the mill and the dried leaves that lay in the river-bed undisturbed. Then the murmur was prolonged, until it became the continuous trouble of some far-off sea, and at last the wind possessed the ledge itself; driving the smoke down the stumpy chimney of the mill, rattling the sun-warped shingles on the roof, stirring the inside rafters with cool breaths, and singing over the rough projections of the outside eaves. At nine o'clock he rolled himself up in his blankets before the fire, as was his wont, and fell asleep.

It was past midnight when he was awakened by the familiar clatter of boulders down the grade, the usual simulation of a wild rush from without that encompassed the whole mill, even to that heavy impact against the door, which he had heard once before. In this he recognized merely the ordinary phenomena of his experience, and only turned over to sleep again. But this time the door rudely fell in upon him, and a figure strode over his prostrate body, with a gun leveled at his head.

He sprang sideways for his own weapon, which stood by the hearth. In another second that action would have been his last, and the solitude of Seth Collinson might have remained henceforward unbroken by any mortal. But the gun of the first figure was knocked sharply upward by a second man, and the one and only shot fired that night sped harmlessly to the roof. With the report he felt his arms gripped tightly behind him; through the smoke he saw dimly that the room was filled with masked and armed men, and in another moment he was pinioned and thrust into his empty armchair. At a signal three of the men left the room, and he could hear them exploring the other rooms and outhouses. Then the two men who had been standing beside him fell back with a certain disciplined precision, as a smooth-chinned man advanced from the open door. Going to the bar, he poured out a glass of whiskey, tossed it off deliberately, and, standing in front of Collinson, with his shoulder against the chimney and his hand resting lightly on his hip, cleared his throat. Had Collinson been an observant man, he would have noticed that the two men dropped their eyes and moved their feet with a half impatient, perfunctory air of waiting. Had he witnessed the stage-robbery, he would have recognized in the smooth-faced man the presence of "the orator." But he only gazed at him with his dull, imperturbable patience.

"We regret exceedingly to have to use force to a gentleman in his own house," began the orator blandly; "but we feel it our duty to prevent a repetition of the unhappy incident which occurred as we entered. We desire that you should answer a few questions, and are deeply grateful that you are still able to do so,—which seemed extremely improbable a moment or two ago." He paused, coughed, and leaned back against the chimney. "How many men have you here besides yourself?"

"Nary one," said Collinson.

The interrogator glanced at the other men, who had reentered. They nodded significantly.

"Good!" he resumed. "You have told the truth—an excellent habit, and one that expedites business. Now, is there a room in this house with a door that locks? Your front door DOESN'T."

"No."

"No cellar nor outhouse?"

"No."

"We regret that; for it will compel us, much against our wishes, to keep you bound as you are for the present. The matter is simply this: circumstances of a very pressing nature oblige us to occupy this house for a few days,—possibly for an indefinite period. We respect the sacred rites of hospitality too much to turn you out of it; indeed, nothing could be more distasteful to our feelings than to have you, in your own person, spread such a disgraceful report through the chivalrous Sierras. We must therefore keep you a close prisoner,—open, however, to an offer. It is this: we propose to give you five hundred dollars for this property as it stands, provided that you leave it, and accompany a pack-train which will start to-morrow morning for the lower valley as far as Thompson's Pass, binding yourself to quit the State for three months and keep this matter a secret. Three of these gentlemen will go with you. They will point out to you your duty; their shotguns will apprise you of any dereliction from it. What do you say?"

"Who yer talking to?" said Collinson in a dull voice.

"You remind us," said the orator suavely, "that we have not yet the pleasure of knowing."

"My name's Seth Collinson."

There was a dead silence in the room, and every eye was fixed upon the two men. The orator's smile slightly stiffened.

"Where from?" he continued blandly.

"Mizzouri."

"A very good place to go back to,—through Thompson's Pass. But you haven't answered our proposal."

"I reckon I don't intend to sell this house, or leave it," said Collinson simply.

"I trust you will not make us regret the fortunate termination of your little accident, Mr. Collinson," said the orator with a singular smile. "May I ask why you object to selling out? Is it the figure?"

"The house isn't mine," said Collinson deliberately. "I built this yer house for my wife wot I left in Mizzouri. It's hers. I kalkilate to keep it, and live in it ontil she comes fur it! And when I tell ye that she is dead, ye kin reckon just what chance ye have of ever gettin' it."

There was an unmistakable start of sensation in the room, followed by a silence so profound that the moaning of the wind on the mountain-side was distinctly heard. A well-built man, with a mask that scarcely concealed his heavy mustachios, who had been standing with his back to the orator in half contemptuous patience, faced around suddenly and made a step forward as if to come between the questioner and questioned. A voice from the corner ejaculated, "By G—d!"

"Silence," said the orator sharply. Then still more harshly he turned to the others "Pick him up, and stand him outside with a guard; and then clear out, all of you!"

The prisoner was lifted up and carried out; the room was instantly cleared; only the orator and the man who had stepped forward remained. Simultaneously they drew the masks from their faces, and stood looking at each other. The orator's face was smooth and corrupt; the full, sensual lips wrinkled at the corners with a sardonic humor; the man who confronted him appeared to be physically and even morally his superior, albeit gloomy and discontented in expression.

He cast a rapid glance around the room, to assure himself that they were alone; and then, straightening his eyebrows as he backed against the chimney, said:—

"D—d if I like this, Chivers! It's your affair; but it's mighty low-down work for a man!"

"You might have made it easier if you hadn't knocked up Bryce's gun. That would have settled it, though no one guessed that the cur was her husband," said Chivers hotly.

"If you want it settled THAT WAY, there's still time," returned the other with a slight sneer. "You've only to tell him that you're the man that ran away with his wife, and you'll have it out together, right on the ledge at twelve paces. The boys will see you through. In fact," he added, his sneer deepening, "I rather think it's what they're expecting."

"Thank you, Mr. Jack Riggs," said Chivers sardonically. "I dare say it would be more convenient to some people, just before our booty is divided, if I were drilled through by a blundering shot from that hayseed; or it would seem right to your high-toned chivalry if a dead-shot as I am knocked over a man who may have never fired a revolver before; but I don't exactly see it in that light, either as a man or as your equal partner. I don't think you quite understand me, my dear Jack. If you don't value the only man who is identified in all California as the leader of this gang (the man whose style and address has made it popular—yes, POPULAR, by G— d!—to every man, woman, and child who has heard of him; whose sayings and doings are quoted by the newspapers; whom people run risks to see; who has got the sympathy of the crowd, so that judges hesitate to issue warrants and constables to serve them),—if YOU don't see the use of such a man, I do. Why, there's a column and a half in the 'Sacramento Union' about our last job, calling me the 'Claude

Duval' of the Sierras, and speaking of my courtesy to a lady! A LADY!—HIS wife, by G—d! our confederate! My dear Jack, you not only don't know business values, but, 'pon my soul, you don't seem to understand humor! Ha, ha!"

For all his cynical levity, for all his affected exaggeration, there was the ring of an unmistakable and even pitiable vanity in his voice, and a self-consciousness that suffused his broad cheeks and writhed his full mouth, but seemed to deepen the frown on Riggs's face.

"You know the woman hates it, and would bolt if she could,—even from you," said Riggs gloomily. "Think what she might do if she knew her husband were here. I tell you she holds our lives in the hollow of her hand."

"That's your fault, Mr. Jack Riggs; you would bring your sister with her infernal convent innocence and simplicity into our hut in the hollow. She was meek enough before that. But this is sheer nonsense. I have no fear of her. The woman don't live who would go back on Godfrey Chivers—for a husband! Besides, she went off to see your sister at the convent at Santa Clara as soon as she passed those bonds off on Charley to get rid of! Think of her traveling with that d— d fool lawyer all the way to Stockton, and his bonds (which we had put back in her bag) alongside of them all the time, and he telling her he was going to stop their payment, and giving her the letter to mail for him!—eh? Well, we'll have time to get rid of her husband before she gets back. If he don't go easy—well"—

"None of that, Chivers, you understand, once for all!" interrupted Riggs peremptorily. "If you cannot see that your making away with that woman's husband would damn that boasted reputation you make so much of and set every man's hand against us, I do, and I won't permit it. It's a rotten business enough,—our coming on him as we have; and if this wasn't the only God-forsaken place where we could divide our stuff without danger and get it away off the highroads, I'd pull up stakes at once."

"Let her stay at the convent, then, and be d—d to her," said Chivers roughly. "She'll be glad enough to be with your sister again; and there's no fear of her being touched there."

"But I want to put an end to that, too," returned Riggs sharply. "I do not choose to have my sister any longer implicated with OUR confederate or YOUR mistress. No more of that—you understand me?"

The two men had been standing side by side, leaning against the chimney. Chivers now faced his companion, his full lips wreathed into an evil smile.

"I think I understand you, Mr. Jack Riggs, or—I beg your pardon—Rivers, or whatever your real name may be," he began slowly. "Sadie Collinson, the mistress of Judge Godfrey Chivers, formerly of Kentucky, was good enough company for you the day you dropped down upon us in our little house in the hollow of Galloper's Ridge. We were living quite an idyllic, pastoral life there, weren't we?—she and me; hidden from the censorious eye of society and— Collinson, obeying only the voice of Nature and the little birds. It was a happy time," he went on with a grimly affected sigh, disregarding his companion's impatient gesture. "You were young then, waging YOUR fight against society, and fresh—uncommonly fresh, I may say—from your first exploit. And a very stupid, clumsy, awkward exploit, too, Mr. Riggs, if you will pardon my freedom. You wanted money, and you had an ugly temper, and you had lost both to a gambler; so you stopped the coach to rob him, and had to kill two men to get back your paltry thousand dollars, after frightening a whole coach-load of passengers, and letting Wells, Fargo, and Co.'s treasure-box with fifty thousand dollars in it slide. It was a stupid, a blundering, a CRUEL act, Mr. Riggs, and I think I told you so at the time. It was a waste of energy and material, and made you, not a hero, but a stupid outcast! I think I proved this to you, and showed you how it might have been done."

"Dry up on that," interrupted Riggs impatiently. "You offered to become my partner, and you did."

"Pardon me. Observe, my impetuous friend, that my contention is that you—YOU—poisoned our blameless Eden in the hollow; that YOU were our serpent, and that this Sadie Collinson, over whom you have become so fastidious, whom you knew as my mistress, was obliged to become our confederate. You did not object to her when we formed our gang, and her house became our hiding-place and refuge. You took advantage of her woman's wit and fine address in disposing of our booty; you availed yourself, with the rest, of the secrets she gathered as MY mistress, just as you were willing to profit by the superior address of her paramour— your humble servant—when your own face was known to the sheriff, and your old methods pronounced brutal and vulgar. Excuse me, but I must insist upon THIS, and that you dropped down upon me and Sadie Collinson exactly as you have dropped down here upon her husband."

"Enough of this!" said Riggs angrily. "I admit the woman is part and parcel of the gang, and gets her share,—or you get it for her," he added sneeringly; "but that doesn't permit her to mix herself with my family affairs."

"Pardon me again," interrupted Chivers softly. "Your memory, my dear Riggs, is absurdly defective. We knew that you had a young sister in the mountains, from whom you discreetly wished to conceal your real position. We respected, and I trust shall always respect, your noble reticence. But do you remember the night you were taking her to school at Santa Clara,—two nights before the fire,—when you were recognized on the road near Skinner's, and had to fly with her for your life, and brought her to us,—your two dear old friends, 'Mr. and Mrs. Barker of Chicago,' who had a pastoral home in the forest? You remember how we took her in,—yes, doubly took her in,—and kept your secret from her? And do you remember how this woman (this mistress of MINE and OUR confederate), while we were away, saved her from the fire on our only horse, caught the stage-coach, and brought her to the convent?"

Riggs walked towards the window, turned, and coming back, held out his hand. "Yes, she did it; and I thanked her, as I thank you." He stopped and hesitated, as the other took his hand. "But, blank it all, Chivers, don't you see that Alice is a young girl, and this woman is—you know what I mean. Somebody might recognize HER, and that would be worse for Alice than even if it were known what Alice's BROTHER was. G—d! if these two things were put together, the girl would be ruined forever."

"Jack," said Chivers suddenly, "you want this woman out of the way. Well—dash it all!—she nearly separated us, and I'll be frank with you as between man and man. I'll give her up! There are women enough in the world, and hang it, we're partners, after all!"

"Then you abandon her?" said Riggs slowly, his eyes fixed on his companion.

"Yes. She's getting a little too maundering lately. It will be a ticklish job to manage, for she knows too much; but it will be done. There's my hand on it."

Riggs not only took no notice of the proffered hand, but his former look of discontent came back with an ill-concealed addition of loathing and contempt.

"We'll drop that now," he said shortly; "we've talked here alone long enough already. The men are waiting for us." He turned on his heel into the inner room. Chivers remained standing by the chimney until his stiffened smile gave way under the working of his writhing lips; then he turned to the bar, poured out and swallowed another glass of whiskey at a single gulp, and followed his partner with half-closed lids that scarcely veiled his ominous eyes.

The men, with the exception of the sentinels stationed on the rocky ledge and the one who was guarding the unfortunate Collinson, were drinking and gambling away their perspective gains around a small pile of portmanteaus and saddle-bags, heaped in the centre of the room. They contained the results of their last successes, but one pair of saddle-bags bore the mildewed appearance of having been cached, or buried, some time before. Most of their treasure was in packages of gold dust; and from the conversation that ensued, it appeared that, owing to the difficulties of disposing of it in the mountain towns, the plan was to convey it by ordinary pack mule to the unfrequented valley, and thence by an emigrant wagon, on the old emigrant trail, to the southern counties, where it could be no longer traced. Since the recent robberies, the local express companies and bankers had refused to receive it, except the owners were known and identified. There had been but one box of coin, which had already been speedily divided up among the band. Drafts, bills, bonds, and valuable papers had been usually intrusted to one "Charley," who acted as a flying messenger to a corrupt broker in Sacramento, who played the role of the band's "fence." It had been the duty of Chivers to control this delicate business, even as it had been his peculiar function to open all the letters and documents. This he had always lightened by characteristic levity and sarcastic comments on the private revelations of the contents. The rough, ill-spelt letter of the miner to his wife, inclosing a draft, or the more sentimental effusion of an emigrant swain to his sweetheart, with the gift of a "specimen," had always received due attention at the hands of this elegant humorist. But the operation was conducted to-night with business severity and silence. The two leaders sat opposite to each other, in what might have appeared to the rest of the band a scarcely veiled surveillance of each other's actions. When the examination was concluded, and, the more valuable inclosures put aside, the despoiled letters were carried to the fire and heaped upon the coals. Presently the chimney added its roar to the moaning of the distant hillside, a few sparks leaped up and died out in the midnight air, as if the pathos and sentiment of the unconscious correspondents had exhaled with them.

"That's a d—d foolish thing to do," growled French Pete over his cards.

"Why?" demanded Chivers sharply.

"Why?—why, it makes a flare in the sky that any scout can see, and a scent for him to follow."

"We're four miles from any traveled road," returned Chivers contemptuously, "and the man who could see that glare and smell that smoke would be on his way here already."

"That reminds me that that chap you've tied up—that Collinson—allows he wants to see you," continued French Pete.

"To see ME!" repeated Chivers. "You mean the Captain?"

"I reckon he means YOU," returned French Pete; "he said the man who talked so purty."

The men looked at each other with a smile of anticipation, and put down their cards. Chivers walked towards the door; one or two rose to their feet as if to follow, but Riggs stopped them peremptorily. "Sit down," he said roughly; then, as Chivers passed him, he added to him in a lower tone, "Remember."

Slightly squaring his shoulders and opening his coat, to permit a rhetorical freedom, which did not, however, prevent him from keeping touch with the butt of his revolver, Chivers stepped into the open air. Collinson had been moved to the shelter of an overhang of the roof, probably more for the comfort of the guard, who sat cross-legged on the ground near him, than for his own. Dismissing the man with a gesture, Chivers straightened himself before his captive.

"We deeply regret that your unfortunate determination, my dear sir, has been the means of depriving US of the pleasure of your company, and YOU of your absolute freedom; but may we cherish the hope that your desire to see me may indicate some change in your opinion?"

By the light of the sentry's lantern left upon the ground, Chivers could see that Collinson's face wore a slightly troubled and even apologetic expression.

"I've bin thinkin'," said Collinson, raising his eyes to his captor with a singularly new and shy admiration in them, "mebbee not so much of WOT you said, ez HOW you said it, and it's kinder bothered me, sittin' here, that I ain't bin actin' to you boys quite on the square. I've said to myself, 'Collinson, thar ain't another house betwixt Bald Top and Skinner's whar them fellows kin get a bite or a drink to help themselves, and you ain't offered 'em neither. It ain't no matter who they are or how they came: whether they came crawling along the road from the valley, or dropped down upon you like them rocks from the grade; yere they are, and it's your duty, ez long ez you keep this yer house for your wife in trust, so to speak, for wanderers.' And I ain't forgettin' yer ginerel soft style and easy gait with me when you kem here. It ain't every man as could walk into another man's house arter the owner of it had grabbed a gun, ez soft-speakin', ez overlookin', and ez perlite ez you. I've acted mighty rough and low-down, and I know it. And I sent for you to say that you and your folks kin use this house and all that's in it ez long ez you're in trouble. I've told you why I couldn't sell the house to ye, and why I couldn't leave it. But ye kin use it, and while ye're here, and when you go, Collinson don't tell nobody. I don't know what ye mean by 'binding myself' to keep your secret; when Collinson says a thing he sticks to it, and when he passes his word with a man, or a man passes his word with him, it don't need no bit of paper."

There was no doubt of its truth. In the grave, upraised eyes of his prisoner, Chivers saw the certainty that he could trust him, even far more than he could trust any one within the house he had just quitted. But this very certainty, for all its assurance of safety to himself, filled him, not with remorse, which might have been an evanescent emotion, but with a sudden alarming and terrible consciousness of being in the presence of a hitherto unknown and immeasurable power! He had no pity for man who trusted him; he had no sense of shame in taking advantage of it; he even felt an intellectual superiority in this want of sagacity in his dupe; but he still felt in some way defeated, insulted, shocked, and frightened. At first, like all scoundrels, he had measured the man by himself; was suspicious and prepared for rivalry; but the grave truthfulness of Collinson's eyes left him helpless. He was terrified by this unknown factor. The right that contends and fights often stimulates its adversary; the right that yields leaves the victor vanquished. Chivers could even have killed Collinson in his vague discomfiture, but he had a terrible consciousness that there was something behind him that he could not make way with. That was why this accomplished rascal felt his flaccid cheeks grow purple and his glib tongue trip before his captive.

But Collinson, more occupied with his own shortcomings, took no note of this, and Chivers quickly recovered his wits, if not his former artificiality. "All right," he said quickly, with a hurried glance at the door behind him. "Now that you think better of it, I'll be frank with you, and tell you I'm your friend. You understand,—your friend. Don't talk much to those men—don't give yourself away to them;" he laughed this time in absolute natural embarrassment. "Don't talk about your wife, and this house, but just say you've made the thing up with me,—with ME, you know, and I'll see you through." An idea, as yet vague, that he could turn Collinson's unexpected docility to his own purposes, possessed him even in his embarrassment, and he was still more strangely conscious of his inordinate vanity gathering a fearful joy from Collinson's evident admiration. It was heightened by his captive's next words.

"Ef I wasn't tied I'd shake hands with ye on that. You're the kind o' man, Mr. Chivers, that I cottoned to from the first. Ef this house wasn't HERS, I'd a' bin tempted to cotton to yer offer, too, and mebbee made yer one myself, for it seems to me your style and mine would sorter jibe together. But I see you sabe what's in my mind, and make allowance. WE don't want no bit o' paper to shake hands on that. Your secret and your folk's secret is mine, and I don't blab that any more than I'd blab to them wot you've just told me."

Under a sudden impulse, Chivers leaned forward, and, albeit with somewhat unsteady hands and an embarrassed will, untied the cords that held Collinson in his chair. As the freed man stretched himself to his full height, he looked gravely down into the bleared eyes of his captor, and held out his strong right hand. Chivers took it. Whether there was some occult power in Collinson's honest grasp, I know not; but there sprang up in Chivers's agile mind the idea that a good way to get rid of Mrs. Collinson was to put her in the way of her husband's finding her, and for an instant, in the contemplation of that idea, this supreme rascal absolutely felt an embarrassing glow of virtue.

CHAPTER VI

The astonishment of Preble Key on recognizing the gateway into which the mysterious lady had vanished was so great that he was at first inclined to believe her entry THERE a mere trick of his fancy. That the confederate of a gang of robbers should be admitted to the austere recesses of the convent, with a celerity that bespoke familiarity, was incredible. He again glanced up and down the length of the shadowed but still visible wall. There was no one there. The wall itself contained no break or recess in which one could hide, and this was the only gateway. The opposite side of the street in the full moonlight stared emptily. No! Unless she were an illusion herself and his whole chase a dream, she MUST have entered here.

But the chase was not hopeless. He had at least tracked her to a place where she could be identified. It was not a hotel, which she could leave at any moment unobserved. Though he could not follow her and penetrate its seclusion now, he could later—thanks to his old associations with the padres of the contiguous college—gain an introduction to the Lady Superior on some pretext. She was safe there that night. He turned away with a feeling of relief. The incongruity of her retreat assumed a more favorable aspect to his hopes. He looked at the hallowed walls and the slumbering peacefulness of the gnarled old trees that hid the convent, and a gentle reminiscence of his youth stole over him. It was not the first time that he had gazed wistfully upon that chaste refuge where, perhaps, the bright eyes that he had followed in the quaint school procession under the leafy Alameda in the afternoon, were at last closed in gentle slumber. There was the very grille through which the wicked Conchita—or, was it Dolores?—had shot her Parthian glance at the lingering student. And the man of thirty-five, prematurely gray and settled in fortune, smiled as he turned away, and forgot the adventuress of thirty who had brought him there.

The next morning he was up betimes and at the college of San Jose. Father Cipriano, a trifle more snuffy and aged, remembered with delight his old pupil. Ah! it was true, then, that he had become a mining president, and that was why his hair was gray; but he trusted that Don Preble had not forgot that this was not all of life, and that fortune brought great responsibilities and cares. But what was this, then? He HAD thought of bringing out some of his relations from the States, and placing a niece in the convent. That was good and wise. Ah, yes. For education in this new country, one must turn to the church. And he would see the Lady Superior? Ah! that was but the twist of one's finger and the lifting of a latch to a grave superintendent and a gray head like that. Of course, he had not forgotten the convent and the young senoritas, nor the discipline and the suspended holidays. Ah! it was a special grace of our Lady that he, Father Cipriano, had not been worried into his grave by those foolish muchachos. Yet, when he had extinguished a snuffy chuckle in his red bandana handkerchief, Key knew that he would accompany him to the convent that noon.

It was with a slight stirring of shame over his elaborate pretext that he passed the gate of the Sacred Heart with the good father. But it is to be feared that he speedily forgot that in the unexpected information that it elicited. The Lady

Superior was gracious, and even enthusiastic. Ah, yes, it was a growing custom of the American caballeros—who had no homes, nor yet time to create any—to bring their sisters, wards, and nieces here, and—with a dove-like side-glance towards Key—even the young senoritas they wished to fit for their Christian brides! Unlike the caballero, there were many business men so immersed in their affairs that they could not find time for a personal examination of the convent,—which was to be regretted,—but who, trusting to the reputation of the Sacred Heart and its good friends, simply sent the young lady there by some trusted female companion. Notably this was the case of the Senor Rivers,— did Don Preble ever know him?—a great capitalist in the Sierras, whose sweet young sister, a naive, ingenuous creature, was the pride of the convent. Of course, it was better that it was so. Discipline and seclusion had to be maintained. The young girl should look upon this as her home. The rules for visitors were necessarily severe. It was rare indeed—except in a case of urgency, such as happened last night—that even a lady, unless the parent of a scholar, was admitted to the hospitality of the convent. And this lady was only the friend of that same sister of the American capitalist, although she was the one who had brought her there. No, she was not a relation. Perhaps Don Preble had heard of a Mrs. Barker,—the friend of Rivers of the Sierras. It was a queer combination of names. But what will you? The names of Americanos mean nothing. And Don Preble knows them not. Ah! possibly?—good! The lady would be remembered, being tall, dark, and of fine presence, though sad. A few hours earlier and Don Preble could have judged for himself, for, as it were, she might have passed through this visitors' room. But she was gone—departed by the coach. It was from a telegram—those heathen contrivances that blurt out things to you, with never an excuse, nor a smile, nor a kiss of the hand! For her part, she never let her scholars receive them, but opened them herself, and translated them in a Christian spirit, after due preparation, at her leisure. And it was this telegram that made the Senora Barker go, or, without doubt, she would have of herself told to the Don Preble, her compatriot of the Sierras, how good the convent was for his niece.

Stung by the thought that this woman had again evaded him, and disconcerted and confused by the scarcely intelligible information he had acquired, Key could with difficulty maintain his composure. "The caballero is tired of his long pasear," said the Lady Superior gently. "We will have a glass of wine in the lodge waiting-room." She led the way from the reception room to the outer door, but stopped at the sound of approaching footsteps and rustling muslin along the gravel walk. "The second class are going out," she said, as a gentle procession of white frocks, led by two nuns, filed before the gateway. "We will wait until they have passed. But the senor can see that my children do not look unhappy."

They certainly looked very cheerful, although they had halted before the gateway with a little of the demureness of young people who know they are overlooked by authority, and had bumped against each other with affected gravity. Somewhat ashamed of his useless deception, and the guileless simplicity of the good Lady Superior, Key hesitated and began: "I am afraid that I am really giving you too much trouble," and suddenly stopped.

For as his voice broke the demure silence, one of the nearest —a young girl of apparently seventeen—turned towards him with a quick and an apparently irresistible impulse, and as quickly turned away again. But in that instant Key caught a glimpse of a face that might not only have thrilled him in its beauty, its freshness, but in some vague suggestiveness. Yet it was not that which set his pulses beating; it was the look of joyous recognition set in the parted lips and sparkling eyes, the glow of childlike innocent pleasure that mantled the sweet young face, the frank confusion of suddenly realized expectancy and longing. A great truth gripped his throbbing heart, and held it still. It was the face that he had seen in the hollow!

The movement of the young girl was too marked to escape the eye of the Lady Superior, though she had translated it differently. "You must not believe our young ladies are all so rude, Don Preble," she said dryly; "though our dear child has still some of the mountain freedom. And this is the Senor Rivers's sister. But possibly—who knows?" she said gently, yet with a sudden sharpness in her clear eyes,—"perhaps she recognized in your voice a companion of her brother."

Luckily for Key, the shock had been so sudden and over-powering that he showed none of the lesser symptoms of agitation or embarrassment. In this revelation of a secret, that he now instinctively felt was bound up with his own future happiness, he exhibited none of the signs of a discovered intriguer or unmasked Lothario. He said quietly and coldly: "I am afraid I have not the pleasure of knowing the young lady, and certainly have never before addressed her." Yet he scarcely heard his companion's voice, and answered mechanically, seeing only before him the vision of the girl's bewitching face, in its still more bewitching consciousness of his presence. With all that he now knew, or thought he knew, came a strange delicacy of asking further questions, a vague fear of compromising HER, a quick impatience of his present deception; even his whole quest of her seemed now to be a profanation, for which he must ask her forgiveness. He longed to be alone to recover himself. Even the temptation to linger on some pretext, and wait for her return and another glance from her joyous eyes, was not as strong as his conviction of the necessity of cooler thought and action. He had met his fate that morning, for good or ill; that was all he knew. As soon as he could decently retire, he thanked the Lady Superior, promised to communicate with her later, and taking leave of Father Cipriano, found himself again in the street.

Who was she, what was she, and what meant her joyous recognition of him? It is to be feared that it was the last question that affected him most, now that he felt that he must have really loved her from the first. Had she really seen him before, and had been as mysteriously impressed as he was? It was not the reflection of a conceited man, for Key had not that kind of vanity, and he had already touched the humility that is at the base of any genuine passion. But he would not think of that now. He had established the identity of the other woman, as being her companion in the house in the hollow on that eventful night; but it was HER profile that he had seen at the window. The mysterious brother Rivers might have been one of the robbers,—perhaps the one who accompanied Mrs. Barker to San Jose. But it was plain that the young girl had no complicity with the actions of the gang, whatever might have been her companion's confederation. In the prescience of a true lover, he knew that she must have been deceived and kept in utter ignorance of it. There was no look of it in her lovely, guileless eyes; her very impulsiveness and ingenuousness would have long since betrayed the secret. Was it left for him, at this very outset of his passion, to be the one to tell her? Could he bear to see those frank, beautiful eyes dimmed with shame and sorrow? His own grew moist. Another idea began to haunt him. Would it not be wiser, even more manly, for him—a man over twice her years—to leave her alone with her secret, and so pass out of her innocent young life as chancefully as he had entered it? But was it altogether chanceful? Was there not in her innocent happiness in him a recognition of something in him better than he had dared to think himself? It was the last conceit of the humility of love.

He reached his hotel at last, unresolved, perplexed, yet singularly happy. The clerk handed him, in passing, a business-looking letter, formally addressed. Without opening it, he took it to his room, and throwing himself listlessly on a chair by the window again tried to think. But the atmosphere of his room only recalled to him the mysterious gift he had found the day before on his pillow. He felt now with a thrill that it must have been from HER. How did she convey it there? She would not have intrusted it to Mrs. Barker. The idea struck him now as distastefully as it seemed improbable. Perhaps she had been here herself with her companion—the convent sometimes made that concession to a relative or well-known friend. He recalled the fact that he had seen Mrs. Barker enter the hotel alone, after the incident of the opening door, while he was leaning over the balustrade. It was SHE who was alone THEN, and had recognized his voice; and he had not known it. She was out again to-day with the procession. A sudden idea struck him. He glanced quickly at the letter in his hand, and hurriedly opened it. It contained only three lines, in a large formal hand, but they sent the swift blood to his cheeks.

"I heard your voice to-day for the third time. I want to hear it again. I will come at dusk. Do not go out until then."

He sat stupefied. Was it madness, audacity, or a trick? He summoned the waiter. The letter had been left by a boy from the confectioner's shop in the next block. He remembered it of old,—a resort for the young ladies of the convent. Nothing was easier than conveying a letter in that way. He remembered with a shock of disillusion and disgust that it was a common device of silly but innocent assignation. Was he to be the ridiculous accomplice of a schoolgirl's extravagant escapade, or the deluded victim of some infamous plot of her infamous companion? He could not believe either; yet he could not check a certain revulsion of feeling towards her, which only a moment ago he would have believed impossible.

Yet whatever was her purpose, he must prevent her coming there at any hazard. Her visit would be the culmination of her folly, or the success of any plot. Even while he was fully conscious of the material effect of any scandal and exposure to her, even while he was incensed and disillusionized at her unexpected audacity, he was unusually stirred with the conviction that she was wronging herself, and that more than ever she demanded his help and his consideration. Still she must not come. But how was he to prevent her? It wanted but an hour of dusk. Even if he could again penetrate the convent on some pretext at that inaccessible hour for visitors,—twilight,—how could he communicate with her? He might intercept her on the way, and persuade her to return; but she must be kept from entering the hotel.

He seized his hat and rushed downstairs. But here another difficulty beset him. It was easy enough to take the ordinary road to the convent, but would SHE follow that public one in what must be a surreptitious escape? And might she not have eluded the procession that morning, and even now be concealed somewhere, waiting for the darkness to make her visit. He concluded to patrol the block next to the hotel, yet near enough to intercept her before she reached it, until the hour came. The time passed slowly. He loitered before shop windows, or entered and made purchases, with his eye on the street. The figure of a pretty girl,—and there were many,—the fluttering ribbons on a distant hat, or the flashing of a cambric skirt around the corner sent a nervous thrill through him. The reflection of his grave, abstracted face against a shop window, or the announcement of the workings of his own mine on a bulletin board, in its incongruity with his present occupation, gave him an hysterical impulse to laugh. The shadows were already gathering, when he saw a slender, graceful figure disappear in the confectioner's shop on the block below. In his elaborate precautions, he had overlooked that common trysting spot. He hurried thither, and entered. The object of his search was not there, and he was compelled to make a shamefaced, awkward survey of the tables in an inner refreshment saloon to satisfy himself. Any one of the pretty girls seated there might have been the one who had just entered, but none was the one he sought. He hurried into the street again,—he had wasted a precious moment,—and resumed his watch. The sun had sunk, the Angelus had rung out of a chapel belfry, and shadows were darkening the vista of the Alameda. She had not come. Perhaps she had thought better of it; perhaps she had been prevented; perhaps the whole appointment had been only a trick of some day-scholars, who were laughing at him behind some window. In proportion as he became convinced that she was not coming, he was conscious of a keen despair growing in his heart, and a sickening remorse that he had ever thought of preventing her. And when he at last reluctantly reentered the hotel, he was as miserable over the conviction that she was not coming as he had been at her expected arrival. The porter met him hurriedly in the hall.

"Sister Seraphina of the Sacred Heart has been here, in a hurry to see you on a matter of importance," he said, eyeing Key somewhat curiously. "She would not wait in the public parlor, as she said her business was confidential, so I have put her in a private sitting-room on your floor."

Key felt the blood leave his cheeks. The secret was out for all his precaution. The Lady Superior had discovered the girl's flight,—or her attempt. One of the governing sister-hood was here to arraign him for it, or at least prevent an open scandal. Yet he was resolved; and seizing this last straw, he hurriedly mounted the stairs, determined to do battle at any risk for the girl's safety, and to perjure himself to any extent.

She was standing in the room by the window. The light fell upon the coarse serge dress with its white facings, on the single girdle that scarcely defined the formless waist, on the huge crucifix that dangled ungracefully almost to her knees, on the hideous, white-winged coif that, with the coarse but dense white veil, was itself a renunciation of all human vanity. It was a figure he remembered well as a boy, and even in his excitement and half resentment touched him now, as when a boy, with a sense of its pathetic isolation. His head bowed with boyish deference as she approached gently, passed him a slight salutation, and closed the door that he had forgotten to shut behind him.

Then, with a rapid movement, so quick that he could scarcely follow it, the coif, veil, rosary, and crucifix were swept off, and the young pupil of the convent stood before him.

For all the sombre suggestiveness of her disguise and its ungraceful contour, there was no mistaking the adorable little head, tumbled all over with silky tendrils of hair from the hasty withdrawal of her coif, or the blue eyes that sparkled with frank delight beneath them. Key thought her more beautiful than ever. Yet the very effect of her frankness and beauty was to recall him to all the danger and incongruity of her position.

"This is madness," he said quickly. "You may be followed here and discovered in this costume at any moment!" Nevertheless, he caught the two little hands that had been extended to him, and held them tightly, and with a frank familiarity that he would have wondered at an instant before.

"But I won't," she said simply. "You see I'm doing a

'half-retreat'; and I stay with Sister Seraphina in her room; and she always sleeps two hours after the Angelus; and I got out without anybody knowing me, in her clothes. I see what it is," she said, suddenly bending a reproachful glance upon him, "you don't like me in them. I know they're just horrid; but it was the only way I could get out."

"You don't understand me," he said eagerly. "I don't like you to run these dreadful risks and dangers for"—He would have said "for me," but added with sudden humility—"for nothing. Had I dreamed that you cared to see me, I would have arranged it easily without this indiscretion, which might make others misjudge you. Every instant that you remain here—worse, every moment that you are away from the convent in that disguise, is fraught with danger. I know you never thought of it."

"But I did," she said quietly; "I thought of it, and thought that if Sister Seraphina woke up, and they sent for me, you would take me away with you to that dear little hollow in the hills, where I first heard your voice. You remember it, don't you? You were lost, I think, in the darkness, and I used to say to myself afterwards that I found you. That was the first time. Then the second time I heard you, was here in the hall. I was alone in the other room, for Mrs. Barker had gone out. I did not know you were here, but I knew your voice. And the third time was before the convent gate, and then I knew you knew me. And after that I didn't think of anything but coming to you; for I knew that if I was found out, you would take me back with you, and perhaps send word to my brother where we were, and then"—She stopped suddenly, with her eyes fixed on Key's blank face. Her own grew blank, the joy faded out of her clear eyes, she gently withdrew her hand from his, and without a word began to resume her disguise.

"Listen to me," said Key passionately. "I am thinking only of

YOU. I want to, and WILL, save you from any blame,—blame you do not understand even now. There is still time. I will go back to the convent with you at once. You shall tell me everything; I will tell you everything on the way."

She had already completely resumed her austere garb, and drew the veil across her face. With the putting on her coif she seemed to have extinguished all the joyous youthfulness of her spirit, and moved with the deliberateness of renunciation towards the door. They descended the staircase without a word. Those who saw them pass made way for them with formal respect.

When they were in the street, she said quietly, "Don't give me your arm—Sisters don't take it." When they had reached the street corner, she turned it, saying, "This is the shortest way."

It was Key who was now restrained, awkward, and embarrassed. The fire of his spirit, the passion he had felt a moment before, had gone out of him, as if she were really the character she had assumed. He said at last desperately:—

"How long did you live in the hollow?"

"Only two days. My brother was bringing me here to school, but in the stage coach there was some one with whom he had quarreled, and he didn't want to meet him with me. So we got out at Skinner's, and came to the hollow, where his old friends, Mr. and Mrs. Barker, lived."

There was no hesitation nor affectation in her voice. Again he felt that he would as soon have doubted the words of the Sister she represented as her own.

"And your brother—did you live with him?"

"No. I was at school at Marysville until he took me away. I saw little of him for the past two years, for he had business in the mountains—very rough business, where he couldn't take me, for it kept him away from the settlements for weeks. I think it had something to do with cattle, for he was always having a new horse. I was all alone before that, too; I had no other relations; I had no friends. We had always been moving about so much, my brother and I. I never saw any one that I liked, except you, and until yesterday I had only HEARD you."

Her perfect naivete alternately thrilled him with pain and doubt. In his awkwardness and uneasiness he was brutal.

"Yes, but you must have met somebody—other men—here even, when you were out with your schoolfellows, or perhaps on an adventure like this."

Her white coif turned towards him quickly. "I never wanted to know anybody else. I never cared to see anybody else. I never would have gone out in this way but for you," she said hurriedly. After a pause she added in a frightened tone: "That didn't sound like your voice then. It didn't sound like it a moment ago either."

"But you are sure that you know my voice," he said, with affected gayety. "There were two others in the hollow with me that night."

"I know that, too. But I know even what you said. You reproved them for throwing a lighted match in the dry grass. You were thinking of us then. I know it."

"Of US?" said Key quickly.

"Of Mrs. Barker and myself. We were alone in the house, for

my brother and her husband were both away. What you said seemed to forewarn me, and I told her. So we were prepared when the fire came nearer, and we both escaped on the same horse."

"And you dropped your shoes in your flight," said Key laughingly, "and I picked them up the next day, when I came to search for you. I have kept them still."

"They were HER shoes," said the girl quickly, "I couldn't find mine in our hurry, and hers were too large for me, and dropped off." She stopped, and with a faint return of her old gladness said, "Then you DID come back? I KNEW you would."

"I should have stayed THEN, but we got no reply when we shouted. Why was that?" he demanded suddenly.

"Oh, we were warned against speaking to any stranger, or even being seen by any one while we were alone," returned the girl simply.

"But why?" persisted Key.

"Oh, because there were so many highwaymen and horse-stealers in the woods. Why, they had stopped the coach only a few weeks before, and only a day or two ago, when Mrs. Barker came down. SHE saw them!"

Key with difficulty suppressed a groan. They walked on in silence for some moments, he scarcely daring to lift his eyes to the decorous little figure hastening by his side. Alternately touched by mistrust and pain, at last an infinite pity, not unmingled with a desperate resolution, took possession of him.

"I must make a confession to you, Miss Rivers," he began with the bashful haste of a very boy, "that is"—he stammered with a half hysteric laugh,—"that is—a confession as if you were really a sister or a priest, you know—a sort of confidence to you—to your dress. I HAVE seen you, or THOUGHT I saw you before. It was that which brought me here, that which made me follow Mrs. Barker—my only clue to you—to the door of that convent. That night, in the hollow, I saw a profile at the lighted window, which I thought was yours."

"I never was near the window," said the young girl quickly. "It must have been Mrs. Barker."

"I know that now," returned Key. "But remember, it was my only clue to you. I mean," he added awkwardly, "it was the means of my finding you."

"I don't see how it made you think of me, whom you never saw, to see another woman's profile," she retorted, with the faintest touch of asperity in her childlike voice. "But," she added, more gently and with a relapse into her adorable naivete, "most people's profiles look alike."

"It was not that," protested Key, still awkwardly, "it was only that I realized something—only a dream, perhaps."

She did not reply, and they continued on in silence. The gray wall of the convent was already in sight. Key felt he had achieved nothing. Except for information that was hopeless, he had come to no nearer understanding of the beautiful girl beside him, and his future appeared as vague as before; and, above all, he was conscious of an inferiority of character and purpose to this simple creature, who had obeyed him so submissively. Had he acted wisely? Would it not have been better if he had followed her own frankness, and—

"Then it was Mrs. Barker's profile that brought you here?" resumed the voice beneath the coif. "You know she has gone back. I suppose you will follow?"

"You will not understand me," said Key desperately. "But," he added in a lower voice, "I shall remain here until you do."

He drew a little closer to her side.

"Then you must not begin by walking so close to me," she said, moving slightly away; "they may see you from the gate. And you must not go with me beyond that corner. If I have been missed already they will suspect you."

"But how shall I know?" he said, attempting to take her hand. "Let me walk past the gate. I cannot leave you in this uncertainty."

"You will know soon enough," she said gravely, evading his hand. "You must not go further now. Good-night."

She had stopped at the corner of the wall. He again held out his hand. Her little fingers slid coldly between his.

"Good-night, Miss Rivers."

"Stop!" she said suddenly, withdrawing her veil and lifting her clear eyes to his in the moonlight. "You must not say THAT—it isn't the truth. I can't bear to hear it from YOUR lips, in YOUR voice. My name is NOT Rivers!"

"Not Rivers—why?" said Key, astounded.

"Oh, I don't know why," she said half despairingly; "only my brother didn't want me to use my name and his here, and I promised. My name is 'Riggs'—there! It's a secret—you mustn't tell it; but I could not bear to hear YOU say a lie."

"Good-night, Miss Riggs," said Key sadly.

"No, nor that either," she said softly. "Say Alice."

"Good-night, Alice."

She moved on before him. She reached the gate. For a moment her figure, in its austere, formless garments, seemed to him to even stoop and bend forward in the humility of age and self-renunciation, and she vanished within as into a living tomb.

Forgetting all precaution, he pressed eagerly forward, and stopped before the gate. There was no sound from within; there had evidently been no challenge nor interruption. She was safe.

CHAPTER VII

The reappearance of Chivers in the mill with Collinson, and the brief announcement that the prisoner had consented to a satisfactory compromise, were received at first with a half contemptuous smile by the party; but for the commands of their leaders, and possibly a conviction that Collinson's fatuous cooperation with Chivers would be safer than his wrath, which might not expend itself only on Chivers, but imperil the safety of all, it is probable that they would have informed the unfortunate prisoner of his real relations to his captor. In these circumstances, Chivers's half satirical suggestion that Collinson should be added to the sentries outside, and guard his own property, was surlily assented to by Riggs, and complacently accepted by the others. Chivers offered to post him himself,—not without an interchange of meaning glances with Riggs,—Collinson's own gun was returned to him, and the strangely assorted pair left the mill amicably together.

But however humanly confident Chivers was in his companion's faithfulness, he was not without a rascal's precaution, and determined to select a position for Collinson where he could do the least damage in any aberration of trust. At the top of the grade, above the mill, was the only trail by which a party in force could approach it. This was to Chivers obviously too strategic a position to intrust to his prisoner, and the sentry who guarded its approach, five hundred yards away, was left unchanged. But there was another "blind" trail, or cut-off, to the left, through the thickest undergrowth of the woods, known only to his party. To place Collinson there was to insure him perfect immunity from the approach of an enemy, as well as from any confidential advances of his fellow sentry. This done, he drew a cigar from his pocket, and handing it to Collinson, lighted another for himself, and leaning back comfortably against a large boulder, glanced complacently at his companion.

"You may smoke until I go, Mr. Collinson, and even afterwards, if you keep the bowl of your pipe behind a rock, so as to be out of sight of your fellow sentry, whose advances, by the way, if I were you, I should not encourage. Your position here, you see, is a rather peculiar one. You were saying, I think, that a lingering affection for your wife impelled you to keep this place for her, although you were convinced of her death?"

Collinson's unaffected delight in Chivers's kindliness had made his eyes shine in the moonlight with a doglike wistfulness. "I reckon I did say that, Mr. Chivers," he said apologetically, "though it ain't goin' to interfere with you usin' the shanty jest now."

"I wasn't alluding to that, Collinson," returned Chivers, with a large rhetorical wave of the hand, and an equal enjoyment in his companion's evident admiration of him, "but it struck me that your remark, nevertheless, implied some doubt of your wife's death, and I don't know but that your doubts are right."

"Wot's that?" said Collinson, with a dull glow in his face.

Chivers blew the smoke of his cigar lazily in the still air.

"Listen," he said. "Since your miraculous conversion a few moments ago, I have made some friendly inquiries about you, and I find that you lost all trace of your wife in Texas in '52, where a number of her fellow emigrants died of yellow fever. Is that so?"

"Yes," said Collinson quickly.

"Well, it so happens that a friend of mine," continued Chivers slowly, "was in a train which followed that one, and picked up and brought on some of the survivors."

"That was the train wot brought the news," said Collinson, relapsing into his old patience. "That's how I knowed she hadn't come."

"Did you ever hear the names of any of its passengers?" said Chivers, with a keen glance at his companion.

"Nary one! I only got to know it was a small train of only two wagons, and it sorter melted into Californy through a southern pass, and kinder petered out, and no one ever heard of it agin, and that was all."

"That was NOT all, Collinson," said Chivers lazily. "I saw the train arrive at South Pass. I was awaiting a friend and his wife. There was a lady with them, one of the survivors. I didn't hear her name, but I think my friend's wife called her 'Sadie.' I remember her as a rather pretty woman—tall, fair, with a straight nose and a full chin, and small slim feet. I saw her only a moment, for she was on her way to Los Angeles, and was, I believe, going to join her husband somewhere in the Sierras."

The rascal had been enjoying with intense satisfaction the return of the dull glow in Collinson's face, that even seemed to animate the whole length of his angular frame as it turned eagerly towards him. So he went on, experiencing a devilish zest in this description of his mistress to her husband, apart from the pleasure of noting the slow awakening of this apathetic giant, with a sensation akin to having warmed him into life. Yet his triumph was of short duration. The fire dropped suddenly out of Collinson's eyes, the glow from his face, and the dull look of unwearied patience returned.

"That's all very kind and purty of yer, Mr. Chivers," he said gravely; "you've got all my wife's pints thar to a dot, and it seems to fit her jest like a shoe I picked up t'other day. But it wasn't my Sadie, for ef she's living or had lived, she'd bin just yere!"

The same fear and recognition of some unknown reserve in this trustful man came over Chivers as before. In his angry resentment of it he would have liked to blurt out the infidelity of the wife before her husband, but he knew Collinson would not believe him, and he had another purpose now. His full lips twisted into a suave smile.

"While I would not give you false hopes, Mr. Collinson," he said, with a bland smile, "my interest in you compels me to say that you may be over confident and wrong. There are a thousand things that may have prevented your wife from coming to you,—illness, possibly the result of her exposure, poverty, misapprehension of your place of meeting, and, above all, perhaps some false report of your own death. Has it ever occurred to you that it is as possible for her to have been deceived in that way as for you?"

"Wot yer say?" said Collinson, with a vague suspicion.

"What I mean. You think yourself justified in believing your wife dead, because she did not seek you here; may she not feel herself equally justified in believing the same of you, because you had not sought her elsewhere?"

"But it was writ that she was comin' yere, and—I boarded every train that come in that fall," said Collinson, with a new irritation, unlike his usual calm.

"Except one, my dear Collinson,—except one," returned Chivers, holding up a fat forefinger smilingly. "And that may be the clue. Now, listen! There is still a chance of following it, if you will. The name of my friends were Mr. and Mrs. Barker. I regret," he added, with a perfunctory cough, "that poor Barker is dead. He was not such an exemplary husband as you are, my dear Collinson, and I fear was not all that Mrs. Barker could have wished; enough that he succumbed from various excesses, and did not leave me Mrs. Barker's present address. But she has a young friend, a ward, living at the convent of Santa Luisa, whose name is Miss Rivers, who can put you in communication with her. Now, one thing more: I can understand your feelings, and that you would wish at once to satisfy your mind. It is not, perhaps, to my interest nor the interest of my party to advise you, but," he continued, glancing around him, "you have an admirably secluded position here, on the edge of the trail, and if you are missing from your post to-morrow morning, I shall respect your feelings, trust to your honor to keep this secret, and— consider it useless to pursue you!"

There was neither shame nor pity in his heart, as the deceived man turned towards him with tremulous eagerness, and grasped his hand in silent gratitude. But the old rage and fear returned, as Collinson said gravely:—

"You kinder put a new life inter me, Mr. Chivers, and I wish I had yer gift o' speech to tell ye so. But I've passed my word to the Capting thar and to the rest o' you folks that I'd stand guard out yere, and I don't go back o' my word. I mout, and I moutn't find my Sadie; but she wouldn't think the less o' me, arter these years o' waitin', ef I stayed here another night, to guard the house I keep in trust for her, and the strangers I've took in on her account."

"As you like, then," said Chivers, contracting his lips, "but keep your own counsel to-night. There may be those who would like to deter you from your search. And now I will leave you alone in this delightful moonlight. I quite envy you your unrestricted communion with Nature. Adios, amigo, adios!"

He leaped lightly on a large rock that overhung the edge of the grade, and waved his hand.

"I wouldn't do that, Mr. Chivers," said Collinson, with a concerned face; "them rocks are mighty ticklish, and that one in partiklar. A tech sometimes sends 'em scooting."

Mr. Chivers leaped quickly to the ground, turned, waved his hand again, and disappeared down the grade.

But Collinson was no longer alone. Hitherto his character-istic reveries had been of the past,—reminiscences in which there was only recollection, no imagination, and very little hope. Under the spell of Chivers's words his fancy seemed to expand; he began to think of his wife as she might be now,—perhaps ill, despairing, wandering hopelessly, even ragged and footsore, or—believing HIM dead—relapsing into the resigned patience that had been his own; but always a new Sadie, whom he had never seen or known before. A faint dread, the lightest of misgivings (perhaps coming from his very ignorance), for the first time touched his steadfast heart, and sent a chill through it. He shouldered his weapon, and walked briskly towards the edge of the thick-set woods.

There were the fragrant essences of the laurel and spruce—baked in the long-day sunshine that had encompassed their recesses—still coming warm to his face; there were the strange shiftings of temperature throughout the openings, that alternately warmed and chilled him as he walked. It seemed so odd that he should now have to seek her instead of her coming to him; it would never be the same meeting to him, away from the house that he had built for her! He strolled back, and looked down upon it, nestling on the ledge. The white moonlight that lay upon it dulled the glitter of lights in its windows, but the sounds of laughter and singing came to even his unfastidious ears with a sense of vague discord. He walked back again, and began to pace before the thick-set wood. Suddenly he stopped and listened.

To any other ears but those accustomed to mountain solitude it would have seemed nothing. But, familiar as he was with all the infinite disturbances of the woodland, and even the simulation of intrusion caused by a falling branch or lapsing pine-cone, he was arrested now by a recurring sound, unlike any other. It was an occasional muffled beat—interrupted at uncertain intervals, but always returning in regular rhythm, whenever it was audible. He knew it was made by a cantering horse; that the intervals were due to the patches of dead leaves in its course, and that the varying movement was the effect of its progress through obstacles and underbrush. It was therefore coming through some "blind" cutoff in the thick-set wood. The shifting of the sound also showed that the rider was unfamiliar with the locality, and sometimes wandered from the direct course; but the unfailing and accelerating persistency of the sound, in spite of these difficulties, indicated haste and determination.

He swung his gun from his shoulder, and examined its caps. As the sound came nearer, he drew up beside a young spruce at the entrance of the thicket. There was no necessity to alarm the house, or call the other sentry. It was a single horse and rider, and he was equal to that. He waited quietly, and with his usual fateful patience. Even then his thoughts still reverted to his wife; and it was with a singular feeling that he, at last, saw the thick underbrush give way before a woman, mounted on a sweating but still spirited horse, who swept out into the open. Nevertheless, he stopped in front of her, and called:—

"Hold up thar!"

The horse recoiled, nearly unseating her. Collinson caught the reins. She lifted her whip mechanically, yet remained holding it in the air, trembling, until she slipped, half struggling, half helplessly, from the saddle to the ground. Here she would have again fallen, but Collinson caught her sharply by the waist. At his touch she started and uttered a frightened "No!" At her voice Collinson started.

"Sadie!" he gasped.

"Seth!" she half whispered.

They stood looking at each other. But Collinson was already himself again. The man of simple directness and no imagination saw only his wife before him—a little breathless, a little flurried, a little disheveled from rapid riding, as he had sometimes seen her before, but otherwise unchanged. Nor had HE changed; he took her up where he had left her years ago. His grave face only broadened into a smile, as he held both her hands in his.

"Yes, it's me—Lordy! Why, I was comin' only to-morrow to find ye, Sade!"

She glanced hurriedly around her, "To—to find me," she

said incredulously.

"Sartain! That ez, I was goin' to ask about ye,—goin' to ask about ye at the convent."

"At the convent?" she echoed with a frightened amazement.

"Yes, why, Lordy Sade—don't you see? You thought I was dead, and I thought you was dead,—that's what's the matter. But I never reckoned that you'd think me dead until Chivers allowed that it must be so."

Her face whitened in the moonlight "Chivers?" she said blankly.

"In course; but nat'rally you don't know him, honey. He only saw you onc't. But it was along o' that, Sade, that he told me he reckoned you wasn't dead, and told me how to find you. He was mighty kind and consarned about it, and he even allowed I'd better slip off to you this very night."

"Chivers," she repeated, gazing at her husband with bloodless lips.

"Yes, an awful purty-spoken man. Ye'll have to get to know him Sade. He's here with some of his folks az hez got inter trouble—I'm forgettin' to tell ye. You see"—

"Yes, yes, yes!" she interrupted hysterically; "and this is the Mill?"

"Yes, lovey, the Mill—my mill—YOUR mill—the house I built for you, dear. I'd show it to you now, but you see, Sade, I'm out here standin' guard."

"Are YOU one of them?" she said, clutching his

hand desperately.

"No, dear," he said soothingly,—"no; only, you see, I giv' my word to 'em as I giv' my house to-night, and I'm bound to protect them and see 'em through. Why, Lordy! Sade, you'd have done the same—for Chivers."

"Yes, yes," she said, beating her hands together strangely, "of course. He was so kind to bring me back to you. And you might have never found me but for him."

She burst into an hysterical laugh, which the simple-minded man might have overlooked but for the tears that coursed down her bloodless face.

"What's gone o' ye, Sadie," he said in a sudden fear, grasping her hands; "that laugh ain't your'n—that voice ain't your'n. You're the old Sadie, ain't ye?" He stopped. For a moment his face blanched as he glanced towards the mill, from which the faint sound of bacchanalian voices came to his quick ear. "Sadie, dear, ye ain't thinkin' anything agin' me? Ye ain't allowin' I'm keeping anythin' back from ye?"

Her face stiffened into rigidity; she dashed the tears from her eyes. "No," she said quickly. Then after a moment she added, with a faint laugh, "You see we haven't seen each other for so long—it's all so sudden—so unexpected."

"But you kem here, just now, calkilatin' to find me?" said Collinson gravely.

"Yes, yes," she said quickly, still grasping both his hands, but with her head slightly turned in the direction of the mill.

"But who told ye where to find the mill?" he said, with gentle patience.

"A friend," she said hurriedly. "Perhaps," she added, with a singular smile, "a friend of the friend who told you."

"I see," said Collinson, with a relieved face and a broadening smile, "it's a sort of fairy story. I'll bet, now, it was that old Barker woman that Chivers knows."

Her teeth gleamed rigidly together in the moonlight, like a death's-head. "Yes," she said dryly, "it was that old Barker woman. Say, Seth," she continued, moistening her lips slowly, "you're guarding this place alone?"

"Thar's another feller up the trail,—a sentry,—but don't you be afeard, he can't hear us, Sade."

"On this side of the mill?"

"Yes! Why, Lord love ye, Sadie! t'other side o' the mill it drops down straight to the valley; nobody comes yer that way but poor low-down emigrants. And it's miles round to come by the valley from the summit."

"You didn't hear your friend Chivers say that the sheriff was out with his posse to-night hunting them?"

"No. Did you?"

"I think I heard something of that kind at Skinner's, but it may have been only a warning to me, traveling alone."

"Thet's so," said Collinson, with a tender solicitude, "but none o' these yer road-agents would have teched a woman. And this yer Chivers ain't the man to insult one, either."

"No," she said, with a return of her hysteric laugh. But it was overlooked by Collinson, who was taking his gun from beside the tree where he had placed it, "Where are you going?" she said suddenly.

"I reckon them fellers ought to be warned o' what you heard. I'll be back in a minit."

"And you're going to leave me now—when—when we've only just met after these years," she said, with a faint attempt at a smile, which, however, did not reach the cold glitter of her eyes.

"Just for a little, honey. Besides, don't you see, I've got to get excused; for we'll have to go off to Skinner's or somewhere, Sadie, for we can't stay in thar along o' them."

"So you and your wife are turned out of your home to please Chivers," she said, still smiling.

"That's whar you slip up, Sadie," said Collinson, with a troubled face; "for he's that kind of a man thet if I jest as much as hinted you was here, he'd turn 'em all out o' the house for a lady. Thet's why I don't propose to let on anything about you till to-morrow."

"To-morrow will do," she said, still smiling, but with a singular abstraction in her face. "Pray don't disturb them now. You say there is another sentinel beyond. He is enough to warn them of any approach from the trail. I'm tired and ill—very ill! Sit by me here, Seth, and wait! We can wait here together—we have waited so long, Seth,—and the end has come now."

She suddenly lapsed against the tree, and slipped in a sitting posture to the ground. Collinson cast himself at her side, and put his arm round her.

"Wot's gone o' ye, Sade? You're cold and sick. Listen. Your hoss is just over thar feedin'. I'll put you back on him, run in and tell 'em I'm off, and be with ye in a jiffy, and take ye back to Skinner's."

"Wait," she said softly. "Wait."

"Or to the Silver Hollow—it's not so far."

She had caught his hands again, her rigid face close to his, "What hollow?—speak!" she said breathlessly.

"The hollow whar a friend o' mine struck silver. He'll take yur in."

Her head sank against his shoulder. "Let me stay here," she answered, "and wait."

He supported her tenderly, feeling the gentle brushing of her hair against his cheek as in the old days. He was content to wait, holding her thus. They were very silent; her eyes half closed, as if in exhaustion, yet with the strange suggestion of listening in the vacant pupils.

"Ye ain't hearin' anythin', deary?" he said, with a troubled face.

"No; but everything is so deathly still," she said in a frightened whisper.

It certainly was very still. A singular hush seemed to have slid over the landscape; there was no longer any sound from the mill; there was an ominous rest in the woodland, so perfect that the tiny rustle of an uneasy wing in the tree above them had made them start; even the moonlight seemed to hang suspended in the air.

"It's like the lull before the storm," she said with her strange laugh.

But the non-imaginative Collinson was more practical. "It's mighty like that earthquake weather before the big shake thet dried up the river and stopped the mill. That was just the time I got the news o' your bein' dead with yellow fever. Lord! honey, I allus allowed to myself thet suthin' was happenin' to ye then."

She did not reply; but he, holding her figure closer to him, felt it trembling with a nervous expectation. Suddenly she threw him off, and rose to her feet with a cry. "There!" she screamed frantically, "they've come! they've come!"

A rabbit had run out into the moonlight before them, a gray fox had dashed from the thicket into the wood, but nothing else.

"Who's come?" said Collinson, staring at her.

"The sheriff and his posse! They're surrounding them now. Don't you hear?" she gasped.

There was a strange rattling in the direction of the mill, a dull rumble, with wild shouts and outcries, and the trampling of feet on its wooden platform. Collinson staggered to his feet; but at the same moment he was thrown violently against his wife, and they both clung helplessly to the tree, with their eyes turned toward the ledge. There was a dense cloud of dust and haze hanging over it.

She uttered another cry, and ran swiftly towards the rocky grade. Collinson ran quickly after her, but as she reached the grade he suddenly shouted, with an awful revelation in his voice, "Come back! Stop, Sadie, for God's sake!" But it was too late. She had already disappeared; and as he reached the rock on which Chivers had leaped, he felt it give way beneath him.

But there was no sound, only a rush of wind from the valley below. Everything lapsed again into its awful stillness. As the cloud lifted from where the mill had stood, the moon shone only upon empty space. There was a singular murmuring and whispering from the woods beyond that increased in sound, and an hour later the dry bed of the old mill-stream was filled with a rushing river.

CHAPTER VIII

Preble Key returned to his hotel from the convent, it is to be feared, with very little of that righteous satisfaction which is supposed to follow the performance of a good deed. He was by no means certain that what he had done was best for the young girl. He had only shown himself to her as a worldly monitor of dangers, of which her innocence was providentially unconscious. In his feverish haste to avert a scandal, he had no chance to explain his real feelings; he had, perhaps, even exposed her thwarted impulses to equally naive but more dangerous expression, which he might not have the opportunity to check. He tossed wakefully that night upon his pillow, tormented with alternate visions of her adorable presence at the hotel, and her bowed, renunciating figure as she reentered the convent gate. He waited expectantly the next day for the message she had promised, and which he believed she would find some way to send. But no message was forthcoming. The day passed, and he became alarmed. The fear that her escapade had been discovered again seized him. If she were in close restraint, she could neither send to him, nor could he convey to her the solicitude and sympathy that filled his heart. In her childish frankness she might have confessed the whole truth, and this would not only shut the doors of the convent against him, under his former pretext, but compromise her still more if he boldly called. He waylaid the afternoon procession; she was not among them.

Utterly despairing, the wildest plans for seeing her passed through his brain,—plans that recalled his hot-headed youth, and a few moments later made him smile at his extravagance, even while it half frightened him at the reality of his passion. He reached the hotel heart-sick and desperate. The porter met him on the steps. It was with a thrill that sent the blood leaping to his cheeks that he heard the man say:—

"Sister Seraphina is waiting for you in the sitting-room."

There was no thought of discovery or scandal in Preble Key's mind now; no doubt or hesitation as to what he would do, as he sprang up the staircase. He only knew that he had found her again, and was happy! He burst into the room, but this time remembered to shut the door behind him. He looked eagerly towards the window where she had stood the day before, but now she rose quickly from the sofa in the corner, where she had been seated, and the missal she had been reading rolled from her lap to the floor. He ran towards her to pick it up. Her name—the name she had told him to call her—was passionately trembling on his lips, when she slowly put her veil aside, and displayed a pale, kindly, middle-aged face, slightly marked by old scars of smallpox. It was not Alice; it was the real Sister Seraphina who stood before him.

His first revulsion of bitter disappointment was so quickly followed by a realization that all had been discovered, and his sacrifice of yesterday had gone for naught, that he stood before her, stammering, but without the power to say a word. Luckily for him, his utter embarrassment seemed to reassure her, and to calm that timidity which his brusque man-like irruption might well produce in the inexperienced, contemplative mind of the recluse. Her voice was very sweet, albeit sad, as she said gently:—

"I am afraid I have taken you by surprise; but there was no time to arrange for a meeting, and the Lady Superior thought that I, who knew all the facts, had better see you confidentially. Father Cipriano gave us your address."

Amazed and wondering, Key bowed her to a seat.

"You will remember," she went on softly, "that the Lady Superior failed to get any information from you regarding the brother of one of our dear children, whom he committed to our charge through a—a companion or acquaintance—a Mrs. Barker. As she was armed with his authority by letter, we accepted the dear child through her, permitted her as his representative to have free access to his sister, and even allowed her, as an unattended woman, to pass the night at the convent. We were therefore surprised this morning to receive a letter from him, absolutely forbidding any further intercourse, correspondence, or association of his sister with this companion, Mrs. Barker. It was necessary to inform the dear child of this at once, as she was on the point of writing to this woman; but we were pained and shocked at her reception of her brother's wishes. I ought to say, in justice to the dear child, that while she is usually docile, intelligent, and tractable to discipline, and a devote in her religious feelings, she is singularly impulsive. But we were not prepared for the rash and sudden step she has taken. At noon to-day she escaped from the convent!"

Key, who had been following her with relief, sprang to his feet at this unexpected culmination.

"Escaped!" he said. "Impossible! I mean," he added, hurriedly recalling himself, "your rules, your discipline, your attendants are so perfect."

"The poor impulsive creature has added sacrilege to her

madness—a sacrilege we are willing to believe she did not understand, for she escaped in a religious habit—my own."

"But this would sufficiently identify her," he said, controlling himself with an effort.

"Alas, not so! There are many of us who go abroad on our missions in these garments, and they are made all alike, so as to divert rather than attract attention to any individuality. We have sent private messengers in all directions, and sought her everywhere, but without success. You will understand that we wish to avoid scandal, which a more public inquiry would create."

"And you come to me," said Key, with a return of his first suspicion, in spite of his eagerness to cut short the interview and be free to act,—"to me, almost a stranger?"

"Not a stranger, Mr. Key," returned the religieuse gently, "but to a well-known man—a man of affairs in the country where this unhappy child's brother lives—a friend who seems to be sent by Heaven to find out this brother for us, and speed this news to him. We come to the old pupil of Father Cipriano, a friend of the Holy Church; to the kindly gentleman who knows what it is to have dear relations of his own, and who only yesterday was seeking the convent to"—

"Enough!" interrupted Key hurriedly, with a slight color. "I will go at once. I do not know this man, but I will do my best to find him. And this—this—young girl? You say you have no trace of her? May she not still be here? I should have some clue by which to seek her—I mean that I could give to her brother."

"Alas! we fear she is already far away from here. If she went at once to San Luis, she could have easily taken a train to

San Francisco before we discovered her flight. We believe that it was the poor child's intent to join her brother, so as to intercede for her friend—or, perhaps, alas! to seek her."

"And this friend left yesterday morning?" he said quickly, yet concealing a feeling of relief. "Well, you may depend on me! And now, as there is no time to be lost, I will make my arrangements to take the next train." He held out his hand, paused, and said in almost boyish embarrassment: "Bid me God speed, Sister Seraphina!"

"May the Holy Virgin aid you," she said gently. Yet, as she passed out of the door, with a grateful smile, a characteristic reaction came over Key. His romantic belief in the interposition of Providence was not without a tendency to apply the ordinary rules of human evidence to such phenomena. Sister Seraphina's application to him seemed little short of miraculous interference; but what if it were only a trick to get rid of him, while the girl, whose escapade had been discovered, was either under restraint in the convent, or hiding in Santa Luisa? Yet this did not prevent him from mechanically continuing his arrangements for departure. When they were completed, and he had barely time to get to the station at San Luis, he again lingered in vague expectation of some determining event.

The appearance of a servant with a telegraphic message at this moment seemed to be an answer to this instinctive feeling. He tore it open hastily. But it was only a single line from his foreman at the mine, which had been repeated to him from the company's office in San Francisco. It read, "Come at once—important."

Disappointed as it left him, it determined his action; and as the train steamed out of San Luis, it for a while diverted his attention from the object of his pursuit. In any event, his destination would have been Skinner's or the Hollow, as the point from which to begin his search. He believed with Sister Seraphina that the young girl would make her direct appeal to her brother; but even if she sought Mrs. Barker, it would still be at some of the haunts of the gang. The letter to the Lady Superior had been postmarked from "Bald Top," which Key knew to be an obscure settlement less frequented than Skinner's. Even then it was hardly possible that the chief of the road agents would present himself at the post-office, and it had probably been left by some less known of the gang. A vague idea, that was hardly a suspicion, that the girl might have a secret address of her brother's, without understanding the reasons for its secrecy, came into his mind. A still more vague hope, that he might meet her before she found her brother, upheld him. It would be an accidental meeting on her part, for he no longer dared to hope that she would seek or trust him again. And it was with very little of his old sanguine quality that, travel-worn and weary, he at last alighted at Skinner's. But his half careless inquiry if any lady passengers had lately arrived there, to his embarrassment produced a broad smile on the face of Skinner.

"You're the second man that asked that question, Mr. Key," he said.

"The second man?" ejaculated Key nervously.

"Yes the first was the sheriff of Sierra. He wanted to find a tall, good-looking woman, about thirty, with black eyes. I hope that ain't the kind o' girl you're looking arter—is it? for I reckon she's gin you both the slip."

Key protested with a forced laugh that it was not, yet suddenly hesitated to describe Alice; for he instantly recognized the portrait of her friend, the assumed Mrs. Barker. Skinner continued in lazy confidence:—

"Ye see they say that the sheriff had sorter got the dead wood on that gang o' road agents, and had hemmed 'em in somewhar betwixt Bald Top and Collinson's. But that woman was one o' their spies, and spotted his little game, and managed to give 'em the tip, so they got clean away. Anyhow, they ain't bin heard from since. But the big shake has made scoutin' along the ledges rather stiff work for the sheriff. They say the valley near Long Canyon's chock full o' rock and slumgullion that's slipped down."

"What do you mean by the big shake?" asked Key in surprise.

"Great Scott! you didn't hear of it? Didn't hear of the 'arthquake that shook us up all along Galloper's the other night? Well," he added disgustedly, "that's jist the conceit of them folks in the bay, that can't allow that ANYTHIN' happens in the mountains!"

The urgent telegrams of his foreman now flashed across Key's preoccupied mind. Possibly Skinner saw his concern, "I reckon your mine is all right, Mr. Key. One of your men was over yere last night, and didn't say nothin'."

But this did not satisfy Key; and in a few minutes he had mounted his horse and was speeding towards the Hollow, with a remorseful consciousness of having neglected his colleagues' interests. For himself, in the utter prepossession of his passion for Alice, he cared nothing. As he dashed down the slope to the Hollow, he thought only of the two momentous days that she had passed there, and the fate that had brought them so nearly together. There was nothing to recall its sylvan beauty in the hideous works that now possessed it, or the substantial dwelling-house that had taken the place of the old cabin. A few hurried questions to the foreman satisfied him of the integrity of the property. There had been some alarm in the shaft, but there was no subsidence of the "seam," nor any difficulty in the working. "What I telegraphed you for, Mr. Key, was about something that has cropped up way back o' the earthquake. We were served here the other day with a legal notice of a claim to the mine, on account of previous work done on the ledge by the last occupant."

"But the cabin was built by a gang of thieves, who used it as a hoard for their booty," returned Key hotly, "and every one of them are outlaws, and have no standing before the law." He stopped with a pang as he thought of Alice. And the blood rushed to his cheeks as the foreman quietly continued:—

"But the claim ain't in any o' their names. It's allowed to be the gift of their leader to his young sister, afore the outlawry, and it's in HER name—Alice Riggs or something."

Of the half-dozen tumultuous thoughts that passed through Key's mind, only one remained. It was purely an act of the brother's to secure some possible future benefit for his sister. And of this she was perfectly ignorant! He recovered himself quickly, and said with a smile:—

"But I discovered the ledge and its auriferous character myself. There was no trace or sign of previous discovery or mining occupation."

"So I jedged, and so I said, and thet puts ye all right. But I thought I'd tell ye; for mining laws is mining laws, and it's the one thing ye can't get over," he added, with the peculiar superstitious reverence of the Californian miner for that vested authority.

But Key scarcely listened. All that he had heard seemed only to link him more fatefully and indissolubly with the young girl. He was already impatient of even this slight delay in his quest. In his perplexity his thoughts had reverted to Collinson's: the mill was a good point to begin his search from; its good-natured, stupid proprietor might be his guide, his ally, and even his confidant.

When his horse was baited, he was again in the saddle. "If yer going Collinson's way, yer might ask him if he's lost a horse," said the foreman. "The morning after the shake, some of the boys picked up a mustang, with a make-up lady's saddle on." Key started! While it was impossible that it could have been ridden by Alice, it might have been by the woman who had preceded her.

"Did you make any search?" he inquired eagerly; "there may have been an accident."

"I reckon it wasn't no accident," returned the foreman coolly, "for the riata was loose and trailing, as if it had been staked out, and broken away."

Without another word, Key put spurs to his horse and galloped away, leaving his companion staring after him. Here was a clue: the horse could not have strayed far; the broken tether indicated a camp; the gang had been gathered somewhere in the vicinity where Mrs. Barker had warned them,—perhaps in the wood beyond Collinson's. He would penetrate it alone. He knew his danger; but as a SINGLE unarmed man he might be admitted to the presence of the leader, and the alleged claim was a sufficient excuse. What he would say or do afterwards depended upon chance. It was a wild scheme—but he was reckless. Yet he would go to Collinson's first.

At the end of two hours he reached the thick-set wood that

gave upon the shelf at the top of the grade which descended to the mill. As he emerged from the wood into the bursting sunlight of the valley below, he sharply reined in his horse and stopped. Another bound would have been his last. For the shelf, the rocky grade itself, the ledge below, and the mill upon it, were all gone! The crumbling outer wall of the rocky grade had slipped away into immeasurable depths below, leaving only the sharp edge of a cliff, which incurved towards the woods that had once stood behind the mill, but which now bristled on the very edge of a precipice. A mist was hanging over its brink and rising from the valley; it was a full-fed stream that was coursing through the former dry bed of the river and falling down the face of the bluff. He rubbed his eyes, dismounted, crept along the edge of the precipice, and looked below: whatever had subsided and melted down into its thousand feet of depth, there was no trace left upon its smooth face. Scarcely an angle of drift or debris marred the perpendicular; the burial of all ruin was deep and compact; the erasure had been swift and sure—the obliteration complete. It might have been the precipitation of ages, and not of a single night. At that remote distance it even seemed as if grass were already growing ever this enormous sepulchre, but it was only the tops of the buried pines. The absolute silence, the utter absence of any mark of convulsive struggle, even the lulling whimper of falling waters, gave the scene a pastoral repose.

So profound was the impression upon Key and his human passion that it at first seemed an ironical and eternal ending of his quest. It was with difficulty that he reasoned that the catastrophe occurred before Alice's flight, and that even Collinson might have had time to escape. He slowly skirted the edge of the chasm, and made his way back through the empty woods behind the old mill-site towards the place where he had dismounted. His horse seemed to have strayed into the shadows of this covert; but as he approached him, he was amazed to see that it was not his own, and that a woman's scarf was lying over its side saddle. A wild idea seized him, and found expression in an impulsive cry:—

"Alice!"

The woods echoed it; there was an interval of silence, and then a faint response. But it was HER voice. He ran eagerly forward in that direction, and called again; the response was nearer this time, and then the tall ferns parted, and her lithe, graceful figure came running, stumbling, and limping towards him like a wounded fawn. Her face was pale and agitated, the tendrils of her light hair were straying over her shoulder, and one of the sleeves of her school-gown was stained with blood and dust. He caught the white and trembling hands that were thrust out to him eagerly.

"It is YOU!" she gasped. "I prayed for some one to come, but I did not dream it would be YOU. And then I heard YOUR voice—and I thought it could be only a dream until you called a second time."

"But you are hurt," he exclaimed passionately. "You have met with some accident!"

"No, no!" she said eagerly. "Not I—but a poor, poor man I found lying on the edge of the cliff. I could not help him much, I did not care to leave him. No one WOULD come! I have been with him alone, all the morning! Come quick, he may be dying."

He passed his arm around her waist unconsciously; she permitted it as unconsciously, as he half supported her figure while they hurried forward.

"He had been crushed by something, and was just hanging

over the ledge, and could not move nor speak," she went on quickly. "I dragged him away to a tree, it took me hours to move him, he was so heavy,—and I got him some water from the stream and bathed his face, and blooded all my sleeve."

"But what were you doing here?" he asked quickly.

A faint blush crossed the pallor of her delicate cheek. She looked away quickly. "I—was going to find my brother at Bald Top," she replied at last hurriedly. "But don't ask me now—only come quick, do."

"Is the wounded man conscious? Did you speak with him? Does he know who you are?" asked Key uneasily.

"No! he only moaned a little and opened his eyes when I dragged him. I don't think he even knew what had happened."

They hurried on again. The wood lightened suddenly. "Here!" she said in a half whisper, and stepped timidly into the open light. Only a few feet from the fatal ledge, against the roots of a buckeye, with HER shawl thrown over him, lay the wounded man.

Key started back. It was Collinson!

His head and shoulders seemed uninjured; but as Key lifted the shawl, he saw that the long, lank figure appeared to melt away below the waist into a mass of shapeless and dirty rags. Key hurriedly replaced the shawl, and, bending over him, listened to his hurried respiration and the beating of his heart. Then he pressed a drinking-flask to his lips. The spirit seemed to revive him; he slowly opened his eyes. They fell upon Key with quick recognition. But the look changed; one could see that he was trying to rise, but that no movement of the limbs accompanied that effort of will, and his old patient, resigned look returned. Key shuddered. There was some injury to the spine. The man was paralyzed.

"I can't get up, Mr. Key," he said in a faint but untroubled voice, "nor seem to move my arms, but you'll just allow that I've shook hands with ye—all the same."

"How did this happen?" said Key anxiously.

"Thet's wot gets me! Sometimes I reckon I know, and sometimes I don't. Lyin' thar on thet ledge all last night, and only jest able to look down into the old valley, sometimes it seemed to me ez if I fell over and got caught in the rocks trying to save my wife; but then when I kem to think sensible, and know my wife wasn't there at all, I get mystified. Sometimes I think I got ter thinkin' of my wife only when this yer young gal thet's bin like an angel to me kem here and dragged me off the ledge, for you see she don't belong here, and hez dropped on to me like a sperrit."

"Then you were not in the house when the shock came?" said Key.

"No. You see the mill was filled with them fellers as the sheriff was arter, and it went over with 'em—and I"—

"Alice," said Key, with a white face, "would you mind going to my horse, which you will find somewhere near yours, and bringing me a medicine case from my saddle-bags?"

The innocent girl glanced quickly at her companion, saw the change in his face, and, attributing it to the imminent danger of the injured man, at once glided away. When she was out of hearing, Key leaned gravely over him:—

"Collinson, I must trust you with a secret. I am afraid that this poor girl who helped you is the sister of the leader of that gang the sheriff was in pursuit of. She has been kept in perfect ignorance of her brother's crimes. She must NEVER know them—nor even know his fate! If he perished utterly in this catastrophe, as it would seem—it was God's will to spare her that knowledge. I tell you this, to warn you in anything you say before her. She MUST believe, as I shall try to make her believe, that he has gone back to the States—where she will perhaps, hereafter, believe that he died. Better that she should know nothing—and keep her thought of him unchanged."

"I see—I see—I see, Mr. Key," murmured the injured man. "Thet's wot I've been sayin' to myself lyin' here all night. Thet's wot I bin sayin' o' my wife Sadie,—her that I actooally got to think kem back to me last night. You see I'd heerd from one o' those fellars that a woman like unto her had been picked up in Texas and brought on yere, and that mebbe she was somewhar in Californy. I was that foolish—and that ontrue to her, all the while knowin', as I once told you, Mr. Key, that ef she'd been alive she'd bin yere—that I believed it true for a minit! And that was why, afore this happened, I had a dream, right out yer, and dreamed she kem to me, all white and troubled, through the woods. At first I thought it war my Sadie; but when I see she warn't like her old self, and her voice was strange and her laugh was strange—then I knowed it wasn't her, and I was dreamin'. You're right, Mr. Key, in wot you got off just now—wot was it? Better to know nothin'—and keep the old thoughts unchanged."

"Have you any pain?" asked Key after a pause.

"No; I kinder feel easier now."

Key looked at his changing face. "Tell me," he said gently,

"if it does not tax your strength, all that has happened here, all you know. It is for HER sake."

Thus adjured, with his eyes fixed on Key, Collinson narrated his story from the irruption of the outlaws to the final catastrophe. Even then he palliated their outrage with his characteristic patience, keeping still his strange fascination for Chivers, and his blind belief in his miserable wife. The story was at times broken by lapses of faintness, by a singular return of his old abstraction and forgetfulness in the midst of a sentence, and at last by a fit of coughing that left a few crimson bubbles on the corners of his month. Key lifted his eyes anxiously; there was some grave internal injury, which the dying man's resolute patience had suppressed. Yet, at the sound of Alice's returning step, Collinson's eyes brightened, apparently as much at her coming as from the effect of the powerful stimulant Key had taken from his medicine case.

"I thank ye, Mr. Key," he said faintly; "for I've got an idea I ain't got no great time before me, and I've got suthin' to say to you, afore witnesses"—his eyes sought Alice's in half apology—"afore witnesses, you understand. Would you mind standin' out thar, afore me, in the light, so I kin see you both, and you, miss, rememberin', ez a witness, suthin' I got to tell to him? You might take his hand, miss, to make it more regular and lawlike."

The two did as he bade them, standing side by side, painfully humoring what seemed to them to be wanderings of a dying man.

"Thar was a young fellow," said Collinson in a steady voice, "ez kem to my shanty a night ago on his way to the—the— valley. He was a sprightly young fellow, gay and chipper-like, and he sez to me, confidential-like, 'Collinson,' sez he,

'I'm off to the States this very night on business of importance; mebbe I'll be away a long time—for years! You know,' sez he, 'Mr. Key, in the Hollow! Go to him,' sez he, 'and tell him ez how I hadn't time to get to see him; tell him,' sez he, 'that RIVERS'—you've got the name, Mr. Key?—you've got the name, miss?—'that RIVERS wants him to say this to his little sister from her lovin' brother. And tell him,' sez he, this yer RIVERS, 'to look arter her, being alone.' You remember that, Mr. Key? you remember it, miss? You see, I remembered it, too, being, so to speak, alone myself"—he paused, and added in a faint whisper—"till now."

Then he was silent. That innocent lie was the first and last upon his honest lips; for as they stood there, hand in hand, they saw his plain, hard face take upon itself, at first, the gray, ashen hues of the rocks around him, and then and thereafter something of the infinite tranquillity and peace of that wilderness in which he had lived and died, and of which he was a part.

Contemporaneous history was less kindly. The "Bald Top Sentinel" congratulated its readers that the late seismic disturbance was accompanied with very little loss of life, if any. "It is reported that the proprietor of a low shebeen for emigrants in an obscure hollow had succumbed from injuries; but," added the editor, with a fine touch of Western humor, "whether this was the result of his being forcibly mixed up with his own tanglefoot whiskey or not, we are unable to determine from the evidence before us." For all that, a small stone shaft was added later to the rocks near the site of the old mill, inscribed to the memory of this obscure proprietor," with the singular legend: "Have ye faith like to him?" And those who knew only of the material catastrophe looking around upon the scene of desolation it commemorated, thought grimly that it must be faith indeed, and—were wiser than they knew.

"You smiled, Don Preble," said the Lady Superior to Key a few weeks later, "when I told to you that many caballeros thought it most discreet to intrust their future brides to the maternal guardianship and training of the Holy Church; yet, of a truth, I meant not YOU. And yet—eh! well, we shall see."

ABOUT THE AUTHOR

 **Francis Bret Harte** (August 25, 1836–May 6, 1902) was an American author and poet, best remembered for his accounts of pioneering life in California.

Born in Albany, New York, Harte moved to California in 1853, later working there in a number of capacities, including miner, teacher, messenger, and journalist. He spent part of his life in the northern California coast town now known as Arcata, at the time it was just a mining camp on Humboldt Bay.

His first literary efforts, including poetry and prose, appeared in The Californian, an early literary journal edited by Charles Henry Webb. In 1868 he became editor of The Overland Monthly, another new literary magazine, but this one more in tune with the pioneering spirit of excitement in California. His story, "The Luck of Roaring Camp," appeared in the magazine's second edition, propelling Harte to nationwide fame.

As an established literary figure, he was appointed to the position of United States Consul in the town of Krefeld, Germany in 1878 and Glasgow in 1880. In 1885 he settled in London. During the thirty years he spent in Europe, he never abandoned writing, and maintained a prodigious output of stories that retained the freshness of his earlier work. He died in England in 1902.

Choose from Thousands of 1stWorldLibrary Classics By

A. M. Barnard	Booth Tarkington	Edward Everett Hale
Ada Leverson	Boyd Cable	Edward J. O'Biren
Adolphus William Ward	Bram Stoker	Edward S. Ellis
Aesop	C. Collodi	Edwin L. Arnold
Agatha Christie	C. E. Orr	Eleanor Atkins
Alexander Aaronsohn	C. M. Ingleby	Eleanor Hallowell Abbott
Alexander Kielland	Carolyn Wells	Eliot Gregory
Alexandre Dumas	Catherine Parr Traill	Elizabeth Gaskell
Alfred Gatty	Charles A. Eastman	Elizabeth McCracken
Alfred Ollivant	Charles Amory Beach	Elizabeth Von Arnim
Alice Duer Miller	Charles Dickens	Ellem Key
Alice Turner Curtis	Charles Dudley Warner	Emerson Hough
Alice Dunbar	Charles Farrar Browne	Emilie F. Carlen
Allen Chapman	Charles Ives	Emily Bronte
Alleyne Ireland	Charles Kingsley	Emily Dickinson
Ambrose Bierce	Charles Klein	Enid Bagnold
Amelia E. Barr	Charles Hanson Towne	Enilor Macartney Lane
Amory H. Bradford	Charles Lathrop Pack	Erasmus W. Jones
Andrew Lang	Charles Romyn Dake	Ernie Howard Pie
Andrew McFarland Davis	Charles Whibley	Ethel May Dell
Andy Adams	Charles Willing Beale	Ethel Turner
Angela Brazil	Charlotte M. Braeme	Ethel Watts Mumford
Anna Alice Chapin	Charlotte M. Yonge	Eugene Sue
Anna Sewell	Charlotte Perkins Stetson	Eugenie Foa
Annie Besant	Clair W. Hayes	Eugene Wood
Annie Hamilton Donnell	Clarence Day Jr.	Eustace Hale Ball
Annie Payson Call	Clarence E. Mulford	Evelyn Everett-green
Annie Roe Carr	Clemence Housman	Everard Cotes
Annonaymous	Confucius	F. H. Cheley
Anton Chekhov	Coningsby Dawson	F. J. Cross
Archibald Lee Fletcher	Cornelis DeWitt Wilcox	F. Marion Crawford
Arnold Bennett	Cyril Burleigh	Fannie E. Newberry
Arthur C. Benson	D. H. Lawrence	Federick Austin Ogg
Arthur Conan Doyle	Daniel Defoe	Ferdinand Ossendowski
Arthur M. Winfield	David Garnett	Fergus Hume
Arthur Ransome	Dinah Craik	Florence A. Kilpatrick
Arthur Schnitzler	Don Carlos Janes	Fremont B. Deering
Arthur Train	Donald Keyhoe	Francis Bacon
Atticus	Dorothy Kilner	Francis Darwin
B.H. Baden-Powell	Dougan Clark	Frances Hodgson Burnett
B. M. Bower	Douglas Fairbanks	Frances Parkinson Keyes
B. C. Chatterjee	E. Nesbit	Frank Gee Patchin
Baroness Emmuska Orczy	E. P. Roe	Frank Harris
Baroness Orczy	E. Phillips Oppenheim	Frank Jewett Mather
Basil King	E. S. Brooks	Frank L. Packard
Bayard Taylor	Earl Barnes	Frank V. Webster
Ben Macomber	Edgar Rice Burroughs	Frederic Stewart Isham
Bertha Muzzy Bower	Edith Van Dyne	Frederick Trevor Hill
Bjornstjerne Bjornson	Edith Wharton	Frederick Winslow Taylor

Friedrich Kerst
Friedrich Nietzsche
Fyodor Dostoyevsky
G.A. Henty
G.K. Chesterton
Gabrielle E. Jackson
Garrett P. Serviss
Gaston Leroux
George A. Warren
George Ade
Geroge Bernard Shaw
George Cary Eggleston
George Durston
George Ebers
George Eliot
George Gissing
George MacDonald
George Meredith
George Orwell
George Sylvester Viereck
George Tucker
George W. Cable
George Wharton James
Gertrude Atherton
Gordon Casserly
Grace E. King
Grace Gallatin
Grace Greenwood
Grant Allen
Guillermo A. Sherwell
Gulielma Zollinger
Gustav Flaubert
H. A. Cody
H. B. Irving
H.C. Bailey
H. G. Wells
H. H. Munro
H. Irving Hancock
H. R. Naylor
H. Rider Haggard
H. W. C. Davis
Haldeman Julius
Hall Caine
Hamilton Wright Mabie
Hans Christian Andersen
Harold Avery
Harold McGrath
Harriet Beecher Stowe
Harry Castlemon
Harry Coghill
Harry Houidini

Hayden Carruth
Helent Hunt Jackson
Helen Nicolay
Hendrik Conscience
Hendy David Thoreau
Henri Barbusse
Henrik Ibsen
Henry Adams
Henry Ford
Henry Frost
Henry James
Henry Jones Ford
Henry Seton Merriman
Henry W Longfellow
Herbert A. Giles
Herbert Carter
Herbert N. Casson
Herman Hesse
Hildegard G. Frey
Homer
Honore De Balzac
Horace B. Day
Horace Walpole
Horatio Alger Jr.
Howard Pyle
Howard R. Garis
Hugh Lofting
Hugh Walpole
Humphry Ward
Ian Maclaren
Inez Haynes Gillmore
Irving Bacheller
Isabel Cecilia Williams
Isabel Hornibrook
Israel Abrahams
Ivan Turgenev
J.G.Austin
J. Henri Fabre
J. M. Barrie
J. M. Walsh
J. Macdonald Oxley
J. R. Miller
J. S. Fletcher
J. S. Knowles
J. Storer Clouston
J. W. Duffield
Jack London
Jacob Abbott
James Allen
James Andrews
James Baldwin

James Branch Cabell
James DeMille
James Joyce
James Lane Allen
James Lane Allen
James Oliver Curwood
James Oppenheim
James Otis
James R. Driscoll
Jane Abbott
Jane Austen
Jane L. Stewart
Janet Aldridge
Jens Peter Jacobsen
Jerome K. Jerome
Jessie Graham Flower
John Buchan
John Burroughs
John Cournos
John F. Kennedy
John Gay
John Glasworthy
John Habberton
John Joy Bell
John Kendrick Bangs
John Milton
John Philip Sousa
John Taintor Foote
Jonas Lauritz Idemil Lie
Jonathan Swift
Joseph A. Altsheler
Joseph Carey
Joseph Conrad
Joseph E. Badger Jr
Joseph Hergesheimer
Joseph Jacobs
Jules Vernes
Julian Hawthrone
Julie A Lippmann
Justin Huntly McCarthy
Kakuzo Okakura
Karle Wilson Baker
Kate Chopin
Kenneth Grahame
Kenneth McGaffey
Kate Langley Bosher
Kate Langley Bosher
Katherine Cecil Thurston
Katherine Stokes
L. A. Abbot
L. T. Meade

L. Frank Baum
Latta Griswold
Laura Dent Crane
Laura Lee Hope
Laurence Housman
Lawrence Beasley
Leo Tolstoy
Leonid Andreyev
Lewis Carroll
Lewis Sperry Chafer
Lilian Bell
Lloyd Osbourne
Louis Hughes
Louis Joseph Vance
Louis Tracy
Louisa May Alcott
Lucy Fitch Perkins
Lucy Maud Montgomery
Luther Benson
Lydia Miller Middleton
Lyndon Orr
M. Corvus
M. H. Adams
Margaret E. Sangster
Margret Howth
Margaret Vandercook
Margaret W. Hungerford
Margret Penrose
Maria Edgeworth
Maria Thompson Daviess
Mariano Azuela
Marion Polk Angellotti
Mark Overton
Mark Twain
Mary Austin
Mary Catherine Crowley
Mary Cole
Mary Hastings Bradley
Mary Roberts Rinehart
Mary Rowlandson
M. Wollstonecraft Shelley
Maud Lindsay
Max Beerbohm
Myra Kelly
Nathaniel Hawthrone
Nicolo Machiavelli
O. F. Walton
Oscar Wilde

Owen Johnson
P.G. Wodehouse
Paul and Mabel Thorne
Paul G. Tomlinson
Paul Severing
Percy Brebner
Percy Keese Fitzhugh
Peter B. Kyne
Plato
Quincy Allen
R. Derby Holmes
R. L. Stevenson
R. S. Ball
Rabindranath Tagore
Rahul Alvares
Ralph Bonehill
Ralph Henry Barbour
Ralph Victor
Ralph Waldo Emmerson
Rene Descartes
Ray Cummings
Rex Beach
Rex E. Beach
Richard Harding Davis
Richard Jefferies
Richard Le Gallienne
Robert Barr
Robert Frost
Robert Gordon Anderson
Robert L. Drake
Robert Lansing
Robert Lynd
Robert Michael Ballantyne
Robert W. Chambers
Rosa Nouchette Carey
Rudyard Kipling
Saint Augustine
Samuel B. Allison
Samuel Hopkins Adams
Sarah Bernhardt
Sarah C. Hallowell
Selma Lagerlof
Sherwood Anderson
Sigmund Freud
Standish O'Grady
Stanley Weyman
Stella Benson
Stella M. Francis

Stephen Crane
Stewart Edward White
Stijn Streuvels
Swami Abhedananda
Swami Parmananda
T. S. Ackland
T. S. Arthur
The Princess Der Ling
Thomas A. Janvier
Thomas A Kempis
Thomas Anderton
Thomas Bailey Aldrich
Thomas Bulfinch
Thomas De Quincey
Thomas Dixon
Thomas H. Huxley
Thomas Hardy
Thomas More
Thornton W. Burgess
U. S. Grant
Upton Sinclair
Valentine Williams
Various Authors
Vaughan Kester
Victor Appleton
Victor G. Durham
Victoria Cross
Virginia Woolf
Wadsworth Camp
Walter Camp
Walter Scott
Washington Irving
Wilbur Lawton
Wilkie Collins
Willa Cather
Willard F. Baker
William Dean Howells
William le Queux
W. Makepeace Thackeray
William W. Walter
William Shakespeare
Winston Churchill
Yei Theodora Ozaki
Yogi Ramacharaka
Young E. Allison
Zane Grey